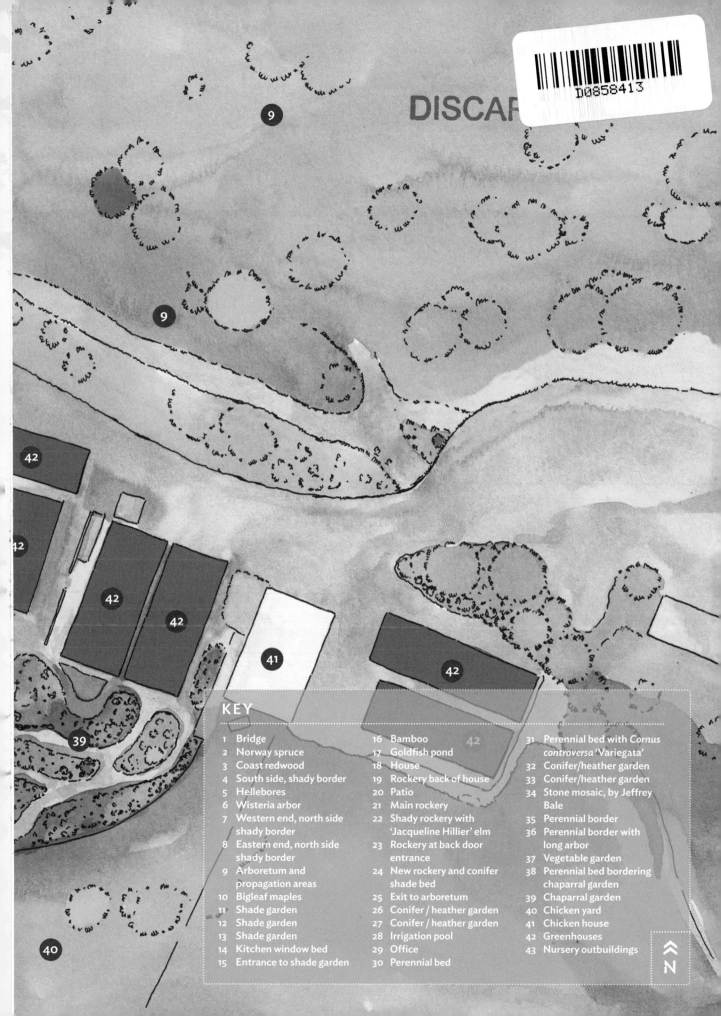

DISCAR

KEY

1 Bridge
2 Norway spruce
3 Coast redwood
4 South side, shady border
5 Hellebores
6 Wisteria arbor
7 Western end, north side shady border
8 Eastern end, north side shady border
9 Arboretum and propagation areas
10 Bigleaf maples
11 Shade garden
12 Shade garden
13 Shade garden
14 Kitchen window bed
15 Entrance to shade garden

16 Bamboo
17 Goldfish pond
18 House
19 Rockery back of house
20 Patio
21 Main rockery
22 Shady rockery with 'Jacqueline Hillier' elm
23 Rockery at back door entrance
24 New rockery and conifer shade bed
25 Exit to arboretum
26 Conifer / heather garden
27 Conifer / heather garden
28 Irrigation pool
29 Office
30 Perennial bed

31 Perennial bed with *Cornus controversa* 'Variegata'
32 Conifer/heather garden
33 Conifer/heather garden
34 Stone mosaic, by Jeffrey Bale
35 Perennial border
36 Perennial border with long arbor
37 Vegetable garden
38 Perennial bed bordering chaparral garden
39 Chaparral garden
40 Chicken yard
41 Chicken house
42 Greenhouses
43 Nursery outbuildings

N

contents

preface

As a young girl in northern Germany, I played farm with little ceramic pigs and sheep and took loving care of cacti and cyclamens on the windowsill. What a thrill it was, watching little seedlings develop from the brown seed capsules of last year's pansies on the balcony. My favorite outings were to the botanical garden, Planten und Bloomen, and the Hagenbeck Zoo in Hamburg.

My family had fled from Pomerania (now Poland) in 1944 when I was two years old to the heath country south of Hamburg with relatives and other refugees toward the close of WWII, and we all lived together on a large estate. My earliest rural memories from that time are of hunting mushrooms, collecting beechnuts, and picking wild blueberries. I clearly recall the excitement and pleasure of gathering food, still a lifelong passion. Five years later we moved to the large city of Hamburg.

As long as I can remember, I yearned for the spaciousness of the countryside. City life, with its man-made environment of stone, asphalt, and cement, oppressed me. Realizing this, my parents offered me a chance at a rural life. Friends of theirs owned Corvey Castle, which had an enormous ancient park and a farm. Their two children were the same age as I. Gladly, I went.

The park, as usual in those days, also contained a large kitchen garden to feed family and staff. We three children were each allocated a little plot to grow anything of our liking. As my two friends were not budding gardeners, I quickly appropriated their plots also. The head gardener provided me with my very first plant starts. So, at age eleven in 1953, I proudly wrote to my parents about the sowed spinach just breaking ground, my six tomato plants, and strawberries that would be put in the next day.

I was allowed to sell my harvest to the head cook, Herr Wanke. (I don't think the strawberries ever made it to the kitchen.) So, I turned proud commercial vegetable gardener at a very early age. Of course, I also grew my first annual sweet peas and marigolds, zinnias and kochias (which were the rage at the time), but those were for the pleasure of beauty only.

At age fourteen, I moved with my parents to Düsseldorf, Germany. In the 1950s America was still regarded in Europe as the land of riches, liberty, and grandeur. For a teenager suffering the constraints of strict European upbringing and schools, America beckoned as the land of freedom. A picture of the Golden

Gate Bridge in all its red splendor hung over my work desk and I wished myself there whenever Latin homework burdened me.

A friend of my father, who was visiting from California, invited me to stay for a year and attend high school in Modesto, then a small agricultural town in the Central Valley. I flew off at age sixteen, with nary a look back, to a wondrous new land.

Not wanting to leave the States after the first year, I entered Monterey Peninsula College, and then transferred to San Francisco State College, where I completed my biology degree. Horticulture, as such, was not offered in western colleges at that time, botany and biology being the closest to it in the natural sciences.

Every weekday for three years, I drove across the Golden Gate Bridge between college in San Francisco and my home in Sausalito, where I lived on a houseboat, a refurbished WWII landing craft, moored next to the sinking wreck of Jack London's original boat, *The Sea Wolf.*

Marietta in the heather.

My gardening experiences were reduced to window boxes and pots on the pier. I turned to birdwatching instead, until I could get my hands into the soil again. My surroundings grew more rural with time, and I left a trail of little gardens behind wherever I lived, from Germany to California to England, where I was married, to Ireland and Greece and finally, to Oregon. I moved often until I arrived in Eugene, and wanted nevermore to leave. I grew roots and they have become deep and strong. It has now been years and the garden is full of old friends—trees, shrubs, bulbs, flowers—and we have memories to share.

Ernie's early childhood was similar in many ways. He also had a very memorable play farm with toy farm animals, tractors, and outbuildings. His family lived in Greeley, Colorado, which at that time was a small community of about 20,000 with streets lined with towering American elms and, though home to Colorado State College, had a very rural farm town feel. It was also home to the largest feedlots in the world at that time. Perhaps as a foreshadowing of a future in animal husbandry, he remembers going with the family touring the feedlots with visitors and having them complain about the smell, but not minding the smell at all. Although most of the extended family stayed in Greeley, his family moved to Palo Alto and eventually to San Diego.

Ernie's early interest in the natural world, especially animals of all kinds, was fostered by his father, who kept snakes and lizards as a child himself, and also by his long-suffering mother, who had learned to be tolerant, since she and

Ernie's father were high school sweethearts and he often carried around bags of snakes. Growing up in San Diego during the '50s and '60s, with property fronting a wild and mainly untouched California chaparral, was a stimulating and heavenly environment for a budding naturalist. At that time there was no compunction about bringing home whatever creatures might be captured and keeping them in terrariums for observation. Many snakes (including rattlesnakes), lizards, scorpions, centipedes, tarantulas, frogs, toads, praying mantises, stick insects, and more were fellow occupants of the bedroom, occasionally escaping, to the chagrin of the family. Most days after school were spent in the canyon exploring, and although many of its denizens were poisonous and Ernie usually went barefoot, his mother just said, "Well, be careful," and he was. The San Diego backcountry was also home to many fascinating plants, such as some showy locoweeds (*Astragalus* spp.), eriogonums (buckwheat), and many interesting flowering shrubs.

Ernie holding king snakes in San Diego where he grew up.

> Ernie in a field of Indian paintbrush, delphiniums, *Artemisia ludoviciana*, and Oregon sunshine, on Iron Mountain in the Willamette National Forest, 2002.

In 1965, he was off to the University of California at Santa Barbara to study biology with views toward becoming a doctor, but after being inspired by a beloved philosophy professor, changed majors and graduated in philosophy and biology.

So, after graduation and deciding not to continue with graduate school, he took some civil service tests and started working for a beautiful public park in Montecito, quickly falling in love with the work and the plants. Some noteworthy memories are of a wisteria covering an arbor walkway over 50 feet long and smothered in bloom every spring, as well as a mature monkey puzzle tree (*Araucaria araucana*) about 100 feet tall, both of which intensified an increasing interest in the plant world. During school at UCSB, many of his vacation days were spent hiking and exploring the Santa Barbara country, visiting the Santa Barbara Botanic Garden, and interest in plants was kindled during those years. At Manning Park, part of his work involved raising on-site many of the perennial and annual display plants. This afforded a good introduction to propagation methods, later useful for nursery efforts in Eugene.

In 1973, when visiting some friends living in Noti to the west of Eugene, they suggested that he look at some property on their road that was for sale. Although he wasn't planning on moving to Oregon, he fell in love with both Oregon and the property, and decided to take the plunge and move north to the 24-acre farm, where he raised goats, calves, hogs, and chickens, and grew a big vegetable garden.

The newly acquired Eugene farm in winter 1973.

beginnings

IN JUNE 1972, my first husband and I and our two small children, Giles and Kimberley, two and four years of age respectively, bought a farm of 70 acres with a farmhouse built in 1918, which lacked many modern amenities except electricity and indoor plumbing. I was attracted to the three magnificent bigleaf maples and two huge Douglas firs that surrounded the house. During the purchase process, we even met the last ancient surviving family member of the original farm homesteaders, who, as a young man, had planted the maples. The most impressive tree on the property was an enormous California black oak (*Quercus kelloggii*), stretching its branches over 100 feet high, with a girth of 23 feet, growing by the old hay barn. When we bought the house we only peered through the windows (the real estate agent had forgotten the key!), and we said, "We'll take it!" I fell in love with the trees at first sight. We didn't even check the soil. We were young, enthusiastic, and horticulturally ignorant.

We also had no idea what it meant to buy an "old farmhouse" on a foundation of oak blocks and stones without a surrounding skirting. The house had totally uninsulated plumbing pipes and single-paned windows with their original glass,

≪previous pages: Northwest Garden Nursery overhead view.

The black oak and the old
hay barn.

Ernie and the old black oak (*Quercus kelloggii*). The oak holds the record as the largest of its
species in Oregon.

Barn owl family, raised in a nest box in the barn.

Our flock of hens, who kept us supplied with eggs.

which afforded a wavy view of the garden. Our first winter, the weather hit an all-time record low for our area, with a temperature of −12°F, and it didn't move above freezing until the spring thaw set in. I awoke one night to the restful sounds of a cascading brook in the forest, but as I became fully conscious, I realized that water from a burst pipe was falling from the second floor through the ceiling and into the downstairs bathtub.

The original chimney burst into flames a few days later. The fireplace had not been used for several years and birds had found it a convenient nesting site, depositing sticks and branches in the open pipe. Once a good hot fire in our newly acquired woodstove took hold (we didn't know yet about chimney sweeps), flames shot out of the chimney, and the nearest wall caught fire. Before the fire department arrived, the fire had been extinguished, not by us, but by our hot water heater that sat below the chimney. The weld on the copper pipes melted from the heat, and water under pressure shot out from the heater and extinguished the blaze, leaving us with a charred wall but an intact house. It seems we innocents led a charmed life.

The farm acreage consisted of open meadows and a recently logged, mixed forest, mostly of Douglas fir. The magnitude of what we did not know was colossal, but our dreams of all that we would accomplish were greater yet. After four and a half years of farming with little money, the dreams of agrarian life and responsibility became too much for my husband, and he left, never to return.

Needing a means of making my livelihood, I went to the local community college with my somewhat impractical biology degree. When I said, "I want to

A fine harvest of Bosc pears from our sixty-five-year-old tree.

learn something that has to do with plants and enables me to make a living," I was promptly enrolled in their two-year landscaping course.

At about that time, I met Ernie, who would become my lifetime partner and husband. He soon sold his farm and moved in with me, and we set out to learn together. While attending the community college, I spied an advertisement offering a full-time job in a landscaping company. Ernie applied for the job and managed the maintenance route. A short time later, we bought the maintenance route and went into the landscaping business ourselves. Plant societies were invaluable educational guides for us. At home, vegetables were a priority. We wanted to live a healthy life. Ancient pear trees grew on the property with suckers of many years' growth as thick as my arm and a crop of poor little fruits, joined by their ancient apple cousins who, soon after we moved in, succumbed to gravity and crashed to the ground. In addition, three sickly English walnut trees and one healthy Bosc pear (*Pyrus communis* variety) rounded out all that was left of a once-thriving orchard. The old pear tree is pruned yearly and produces abundantly for us and many of our friends.

We had started with the dream of becoming organic farmers, raising sheep, goats, eggs, and produce, but we were ahead of our time. The alternative community (then called hippies) had little money, and for the general population, meat, eggs, and vegetables had no special label—the cheaper the better—but at least our family, with two small children, ate well.

There was no garden to speak of then. I have asked myself many times what it is that drives the two of us to this endless quest for beauty. We toil and sweat, pushing innumerable wheelbarrows, digging holes, planting and pruning, wrestling with unwieldy pots and roots, only stopping when it's too dark to see, so, in summer, we eat dinner at 10 p.m. Others can only see the "hard work." But for us it is a passion, this quest for beauty, and I hope it never leaves us.

Beneath the big trees and fruit orchard there grew grass—lots of it. The house was surrounded by a meadow, which was listed in the real estate description as "lawn." The only decorative elements consisted of a white picket fence, a dying rose on an arbor, and a drought-stricken rhododendron. Our newly arrived goats promptly defoliated the rhody and then became very sick. We cut this rhododendron, named 'Cynthia', which is one of the old ironclad rhodies, twice to the ground because we disliked its brazen pink flower color. Each time it resurrected itself. A plant like that commands respect, so we decided to let it be. Each spring it covers itself in pink and now reaches the second story of the house.

Our greatest difficulty in our summer dry climate was an 8-gallon-a-minute well (according to the seller) that turned out to be about a 1-gallon-a-minute well. That is about enough to either water a 4-foot area in the garden or take a short shower. We drilled several more wells, all of them expensive dry holes, and subsequently built a "livestock" pond that leaked in our sandy soil.

In 1975, when we first started farming, we made the ill-advised decision to add two cows and calves to our already unmanageable menagerie. Within a few years, I decided that those obstreperous, large beasts had to go. An ad in the local paper brought us a buyer for one pair. The second buyer offered a trade—cow and calf for a 10,000-gallon aboveground swimming pool. Just what I needed with so little water to spare, but then I needed the cow-calf pair even less. So I said, "It's a deal. Maybe the fire department will fill it for me." And so they did! After that we were on our own. At first the children loved it, then enthusiasm and care of the pool waned and the water turned green, a haven for water insects and trysting tree frogs. But, Ernie, the ever-practical, had the idea of letting the well water flow into the pool at low-use time periods during the night and midday. He fitted the pool with a foot valve and pump, trenched a 500-foot line with eleven faucets through the property for irrigation, and we were off to start our garden paradise.

Araucana rooster.

Eventually, in the 1980s, we were able to drill a somewhat successful well in the woods with the help of an ancient well dowser, but it was a thousand feet from the garden. In the meantime, we worked hard in town maintaining other people's gardens, which had lots of enviable water, and we brought home their drought-tolerant discards to plant on the farm. Junipers and mugo pines were the most common "gifts."

An empty slate is not necessarily a bad thing, and our gardening trials began. Fencing our goats and sheep in, or better, out, away from the house, became an obvious necessity after our newly acquired billy goat, in a panic attack caused by a curious dog, jumped through the kitchen window and landed in a rain of glass on the dining room table. Grazing sheep and goats and growing a garden are not compatible without a sturdy fence.

Our next project was to screen the house from the road. Not many cars pass by on our country road in the foothills of Oregon's Coast Range, but a view of greenery is preferable to a view of a road. At least it gives you the pretense of being away from it all. We decided on a bamboo hedge. With the knowledge of plants I have now, would I have dared to screen the whole length of the 150-foot road frontage and south side of the garden with a running bamboo? I think not. Yet it has been highly successful and, after forty years and a bit of trenching to limit its exuberant runners, it has become our 20-foot-high curtain from the outside world, evergreen and swaying with the wind. It is now the sleeping quarters for many types of birds that chirp and twitter as they roost each night in summer. We leave sections along the road unthinned for greater leaf density as cover, and those to the south of us we thin out to enjoy the graceful structure of the naked bamboo culms.

Under the maples in the lawn meadow in front of the house, I dreamt of creating a romantic woodland garden. A gravel path surrounding the house would be first.

Before Ernie's arrival, I was the only gardener in the family, and I built a good set of biceps shoveling and wheeling endless barrows of gravel for paths. Fortunately, we live on level ground. Then I ordered great multitudes of dormant ostrich ferns from a mail-order nursery, dug holes, and tossed into each a bit of 16-16-16 commercial fertilizer. I also lovingly surrounded them with a bit more fertilizer, and, to top it off, sprinkled some on the crown of each. They did not take long to die, or cook to death, from fertilizer burn. That was my first lesson in commercial fertilizer. I learned to go organic in the garden in the early 1970s even though it was still considered an eccentric fad.

Going through old photographs I now realize how changed our garden landscape is from its beginnings. Gardening is not like painting a picture. When a painting is finished, it stays as is, but a garden canvas gets repainted with every growing season. What are now our perennial borders had their start as a meadow, then a well-enriched vegetable garden, which eventually morphed into a flower paradise of mainly giant dahlias and roses. Trees and shrubs were added later, grew larger over time, and have now become a mixed sunny-shady border. I often meet people who would love to beautify their surroundings by starting a garden, yet they feel intimidated by the possibility of making mistakes.

> The large *Rhododendron* 'Cynthia', with *Hydrangea quercifolia*.

My first flower garden, in 1974, behind our house, guarded by our Irish wolfhound, Sixpence.

Be of good courage; we all start that way. Even the most sophisticated garden was once an empty lot or meadow.

Many regions of the world have contributed to the diversity of our garden. Varied environments that once covered the world—the unending prairies, woodlands, and alpine landscapes—have become small islands of imagination, sized down to a mere garden of 2 acres. The shady woodland dell, the ethereal alpine region, the flowering wild meadow of the subalpine landscape, the chaparral, dry, tough, and spiky, and the wild, low heaths embroidered with shrubs and conifers—all have become garden microcosms, just slightly tamer but vibrant versions of their wild ancestors.

It is easy to forget how much horticultural knowledge and plant availability have increased in the past thirty years. In Oregon, plant societies and seminars were just getting started in the early 1980s. Retail nurseries mostly carried annuals, vegetables, and the standard foundation plants like azaleas, large-flowered rhododendrons, and photinias. We now live in a much more diverse plant world. We become overwhelmed each year with new varieties that have been produced at dizzying speed. What choices we have!

< Bamboo screen, *Phyllostachys nigra* f. *henonis*.

the vegetable and fruit garden

ALONG WITH OUR early attempts at ornamental gardening, we wanted to be as self-sufficient as possible where food was concerned. The two goats already produced our milk, sheep and chickens gave us meat and eggs, and later a couple of pigs rounded out our farm, along with the many varieties of vegetables that we began to grow. We derive enormous satisfaction from growing a portion of our own food. Certainly we will never be totally self-sufficient. Some of our meat is grown by a neighbor, and we fetch oil, rice, butter, and chocolate from the store, but there is much we can contribute to our food supply, even with a small garden.

To start a serious vegetable garden, we hired a farmer friend with her own giant rototiller to till up some of the meadow. We had become devoted readers about organic gardening, and knew the solution to lack of water and fertility was mulch and lots of it. We dreamt big, which meant scouring the surrounding area for mulch. We found our soil to be sandy and silty, low in nutrition and humus, with excellent drainage—too excellent, actually, because it did not hold water well at all. Farms around us supplied us with manure from their cows, llamas, and chickens, and our animals did their part. We begged for spoiled alfalfa and wheat

< *Diospyros* ×'Nikita's Gift'.

There is nothing sweeter than homegrown asparagus ('Jersey Giant', a sterile male variety), well-fertilized with a yearly straw and manure mulch.

Swiss chard.

Broccoli.

Black figs (*Ficus* 'Negronne').

Late summer and fall are harvest time in the Pacific Northwest.

straw, which we layered between the veggie rows to good effect, both as a weed suppressor and for soil improvement. After one mistake, we learned never to accept spoiled hay or manure with hay in it, after a luxuriant grass crop sprouted among our vegetables in early spring. All the leaves from our trees went on top of the soil in the veggie garden in fall, a practice we still follow to this day. Organic supplements such as fishmeal are still used when planting new rows of vegetables. For many years we rototilled all the mulch material into the soil once in early spring. Often this became a rather hazardous activity, especially in cloudy, cool weather. We were raising honeybees in five hives at the edge of the vegetable garden. Bees lacking nectar activity because of cool weather become very grumpy. They buzzed in front of my face and got tangled in my hair, all because they regarded the noisy rototiller as a predatory threat.

Now, after forty years of rototilling and mulching, the soil is so alive with bacteria, fungi, insects, and other arthropods, worms, moles, and voles, that tilling is no longer necessary. Even the 1-foot-layer of leaves applied each winter miraculously disappears by midsummer. A slug bait acceptable to organic vegetable gardeners in the form of iron sulphate, Sluggo, has become a necessary bait in spring since slugs and snails also love a cool, damp leaf mulch. All I do is cultivate a row wherever I place seeds or little starts. Instead of building a compost pile of kitchen scraps that needs continual turning, we take the easy way out and, after dogs and chickens get their share, we bury the rest under the soil. It disappears in no time at all, or I should say it is converted into more rich compost as food for a new generation of edibles.

I have seen attractive vegetable and fruit gardens designed specially to please the eye with patterns and color. For me a vegetable garden's function is to please the stomach, especially mine and our family and guests'. It exists to feed us all year long. There is nothing more satisfying than gloating over that six-dollar-per-pound asparagus at the organic grocer when you can go home and cut the sweetest green tips to cook and eat, only minutes after harvest, with a fresh chervil butter sauce.

Leafy vegetables, backed here by a curtain of asparagus in fall. The asparagus must not be cut back until frosted and brown in winter.

Summer brings a wealth of daily harvest in the vegetable and fruit garden. Lettuce, broccoli, zucchini, beets, sorrel, and mache are the delights. After July days, when we eagerly fondled each orange-colored tomato to check for ripeness, finally the first tomatoes are ripe, an endless stream of them, and then

Italian sweet red peppers. We roast both tomatoes and peppers with plenty of homegrown garlic, onions, and fresh basil, and olive oil, and we freeze the surplus. Winter pizzas and pastas will be covered with generous helpings of tomato sauce and grilled peppers. Memories of summer are rekindled with meals of fragrant dishes in bleak January.

Late summer and early fall are harvest time in the Pacific Northwest. Beginning in August, gardeners wait for the gentle breezes of fall that bring with them the first brief rain showers. A pattering of raindrops on the window in the middle of the night is a much-welcomed sound. Did you hear that? Is that really rain? What a pleasant relief, a respite from dragging hoses for three months or more. The still warm days and cooling showers bring an abundance of ripening fruits and vegetables that must be stored for winter, may it be by freezing, canning, or dark, dry storage, or to be taken to the local food pantry. Potatoes and onions and later harvested squash are all stored in our generous pantry (most old farmhouses have a large storage room.)

Strawberries, raspberries, blackberries, grapes, currants, and figs are favorite fruits. What can't be eaten fresh is converted into juice and jam or frozen for winter and spring. In days long gone by, our two school-age children complained, "Raspberries again! Why can't we have oranges like the other kids in school?" These complaints went along with those about homemade bread. Life can be tough.

We grow Bartlett pears for canning with a syrup of honey, cloves, and ginger, a Bosc pear for sweet eating, and the late and tastiest d'Anjou and Comice pears for flavor and excellent storage ability into winter, if stored cool but frost-free. Our giant, aged, Gravenstein apple tree provides more than we could ever eat or turn into applesauce.

When my mother visited, on viewing all my rows and rows of canned fruit, she compared us to busy squirrels, stashing nuts in fall. I confess that I attain an enormous satisfaction from all this plenty stored for the cold part of the year. And like squirrels, when the first new greens and asparagus sprouts of spring appear, we have usually consumed the bounty of the previous year.

Some vegetables live all winter in the ground in the relatively mild Pacific Coast climate. Leeks, parsnips, carrots, kale, and celeriac handle frosts well, but any root vegetable may also be a winter meal for ever-active voles, leading to a harvest of wilted carrot or parsnip tops with nary a root attached.

Our vegetable and fruit garden used to be an immense 6,000 square feet, but it has shrunk now to about 2,100 square feet as our productivity increased and our family decreased after the children left for college and it was only the two of us. We learned to shorten the rows of beans, peas, and lettuces. We began to repeat-plant in three-week intervals to ensure a continuous supply of any vegetable that goes to seed quickly. The rest of the vegetable garden with its now rich soil was converted into perennial borders.

> View along the poplar alleé toward the woods.

the
shade
garden

THE SUCCESS OF ornamental gardening lies in creating an illusion. The garden visitor is led to believe that the multitude of ground covers growing cheek by jowl are living in happy harmony, when actually they would really like nothing better than to overwhelm their neighbor. One of the skills, then, is choosing which plants can be kept in bounds and not kill their growing companions. Of course, sometimes we fail in this endeavor. We constantly edit with shears, spade, and clippers. I have heard these words so often: "Oh! That must be so much work" (the word "work" usually accompanied with an audible sigh implying "drudgery"). But we love what we are doing and get enormous satisfaction from an accomplished task and the pleasing result.

Neither I nor Ernie is interested in "low-maintenance gardening," with orderly shrubs, surrounded by chipped mulch, and plants that don't touch, or a garden in which Darwin's evolutionary theory has quite literally taken hold and the mightiest plant has overtaken most of the other plants on the way to becoming the sole possessor of the land.

< *Pieris japonica* 'Flaming Silver' surrounded by groundcovers of pulmonaria, *Ranunculus ficaria* 'Brazen Hussy', and *Anemone nemorosa* in April.

Ernie installed a large shady border along our bamboo hedge and bisected it with a stone path. Here he is hard at work in the 1980s.

The shady stone path, thirty years later, with *Taxodium distichum* 'Pendulum' and *Aralia elata* 'Variegata'.

"I have so much shade I can't grow anything" is a common complaint among gardeners. When we were landscapers in the 1980s, rhododendrons and azaleas with bark mulch as ground cover were the prevalent solution of many garden professionals. Shade was seen as a problem, not as a gardening opportunity. Now I hunt for more shade, since so many desirable shade treasures crowd catalogs, nurseries, and plant seminars. But, let me not get ahead of myself.

In the early 1980s, Ernie and I set to work curtailing the lawn, edging the shady front garden on one side with an undulating border of cement about 4 inches wide abutting an open area of river gravel fronting the house. The ground just around the maples was too dry for anything but spring bulbs. We planted the beds with hundreds of red tulips and countless crocus and scilla. It was a grand spring celebration, ever multiplying for about twenty years, until one day an adventurous mole tunneled through yards of dry gravel followed by hordes of ever-hungry meadow voles. Within two years all those many bulbs disappeared, an invisible underground feast, leaving only grape hyacinths behind. Over the years a few crocus and daffodils reappeared.

As our bamboo screen grew and the maples spread their already large canopy, we added some young Douglas firs to the area because we love trees. Little conifers have a tendency to grow larger though and some eventually were cut. Three were blown over in a windstorm.

We wanted to install a shady border along our bamboo hedge bisected by a paved stone and chip woodland path. Our impatience to plant was tempered by the lessons learned during the landscaping courses in college as well as our impressive results in the edible garden plots. We needed to amend the soil first! So, we brought in many truckloads of compost to enrich future plantings and hang on to any precious water in summer. I have seen too many rhododendron gardens speedily planted and then exploding in a cacophony of mismatched colors in April and May and then subsiding into indifferent blobs of shrubbery for the rest of the season. We did not want to repeat that approach. Yes, we did plant rhododendrons, but with moderation and insisting on good foliage.

With growing exposure to the world of beautiful plants, we became collectors, wanting to grow whatever struck our fancy. We wanted to blend our collectors' urges with our desire for a good design, plants with foliage that varied from coarse to lacy, from ground cover level to tall shrubs and small trees, to maintain our visual interest and fascination with our garden and surroundings all year long. A collector needs room for onesies and twosies of ever-precious rarities.

Early on, before the age of computers, Ernie decided to keep track of all newly purchased plants with their exact garden locations noted down on 4-by-6-inch index cards and with the intention of following and recording their source and habits. It was a short-lived obsession as the rate of plant acquisition overwhelmed organizational skills and time.

I realize now that perfection can never be achieved, and plants can be pruned, moved, or even discarded to the compost heap with the help of a wheelbarrow. A garden is a truly movable feast as Ernie discovered when he often saw the wheelbarrows, with plants bouncing, trundling by his office window destined for a new home and threatening his orderly notations.

The shade garden is visible from our living room and kitchen on the west and north sides of the house. We have big windows through which we watch the changing seasons. The house and garden are no longer visible from the road; the bamboo acts like a giant curtain across a stage. Only when visitors enter through the gate does the front garden open up to the viewer. It is like entering another country, a hidden world away from the world at large, even though the house is actually quite close to our country road.

Our walk through the shade garden begins at the southeast end of the wall of bamboo. A narrow path of wood chips winds its way between the plantings. As a child, I liked to wander in the woods by myself, trying to find that secret path or nook no one else had discovered. As an adult, I found that same magic of discovery in the old-growth forests of the Pacific Northwest, and I try to recreate this sense of mystery in a smaller form in our garden. A walk here is always a fresh journey of surprise and discovery. What lies around the next corner? Our paths are laid out so that the end is not quite in sight.

A weeping bald cypress (*Taxodium distichum* 'Pendulum') hides some shade-demanding (not simply shade-tolerant) treasures under its pendulous branches, which are soft green in summer, golden brown in fall, and bare in winter. Several *Arisaema serratum*, with leaves silver-centered and with bright red seed heads in fall, huddle underneath it together with tiny, 4-inch-tall, silvery *Paris luquanensis*. Next on the path, left and right, are my favorite exotic shade-loving and wonderful *Aralia elata* 'Variegata', with enormous, thrice-pinnate leaves each the size of a small branch. But there is more. In August, panicles of deliciously scented white flowers appear, mobbed by crazed hordes of honeybees, followed in the fall by tiny, edible blue berries, and as a grand finale, spectacular red-purple-pink-silver fall color. After the "branches" (leaf petioles) fall off we are left with an odd knobby bare tree in winter, ornamental in its own way. Since it was grafted (and therefore, sadly, very expensive), we must pull out the very thorny root suckers, but it's worth the pain.

Paris polyphylla var. *stenophylla*.

The centerpiece of the north shade border is a magnificent forty-eight-year-old contorted filbert tree, *Corylus avellana* 'Contorta'. It is religiously shaped and thinned every winter after it sheds its golden fall foliage. Without pruning, it would deteriorate into a tangled jumble. In spring and summer, trilliums, red 'Volcano' being the most showy, Chinese podophyllums, ferns, and golden lily-of-the-valley (*Convallaria majalis* 'Fernwood Golden Slippers') cover the ground beneath it. Pruning is best done before the golden carpet of hazelnut leaves is raked up in fall, so dormant growth tips of trilliums and mayapples (*Podophyllum* spp.) are not damaged by the pruner's feet and ladder.

Aralia elata 'Variegata' blooming.

Aralia elata 'Variegata' in fruit.

Aralia elata 'Variegata' with black berries in fall.

Ground cover of *Anemone nemorosa* with blue-flowered pulmonarias, epimediums, podophyllums, ferns, and grasses.

Corylus avellana 'Contorta' (Harry Lauder's walking stick) with *Trillium chloropetalum* 'Volcano' below.

Trillium cuneatum under the contorted filbert.

> View past the contorted filbert toward the patio.

A mass of podophyllums covers the beds beyond the contorted filbert, with *Dicentra spectabilis* 'Gold Heart' in the background at left.

Podophyllum pleianthum with flower buds.

Podophyllum hybrid in container.

In February and March, long, elegant catkins dangle on the hazelnut's contorted branches, its showiest time of the year. I like to grow two good conifer genera in these shady spots: *Taxus* (yew) and *Tsuga* (hemlock). Both types of tree are rich in dwarf and yellow-foliaged cultivars. We use *Taxus baccata* 'Summergold' and 'Repens Aurea', *Tsuga canadensis* 'Everitt's Golden' (which is green for us because it gets too much shade), and *Tsuga canadensis* 'Prostrata' to add a different foliage texture to the many podophyllums and trilliums.

I like conifers in the shady mix, as well as evergreen ferns, to provide finely textured, persistent foliage in the predominantly large-leaved abundance in summer and barrenness in winter. Long ago we tried introducing various hostas for large-leaved, colorful effect in dark corners of the garden. But we ended up with a plague of slugs and snails from the meadows around us, and ugly shredded leaves despite lots of baiting and nighttime raids with bucket and clippers. Then, we discovered the southwestern Chinese mayapple species, belonging to the family Berberidaceae, which has many alkaloids in their leaves that give them slug resistance. We first saw a sample of *Podophyllum delavayi* in the garden of Heronswood Nursery in western Washington, an eye-catching, alien-looking plant with starfish-shaped leaves and odd red

Podophyllum delavayi (left), P. 'Spotty Dotty' (center), and P. 'Red Panda' (right).

and black markings. Weird and wonderful it was, and soon we started to acquire a collection of various species. They make up the element our shade garden was missing: a big, bold, colorful leaf.

Curiosity is never satisfied. Humankind must meddle, and meddle we did. Get out the paintbrush, play the bee, and start crossing the various species of podophyllums—green, large-leaved, and tall paired with those of smaller stature with painted leaves. White marking tags dangle on their dark red flowers to label the crosses. As with hostas, the offspring multiplied, and we planted the best out in the garden until every moist, shady nook is now filled with them.

Continuing the walk in late spring, we come upon a mayapple gathering. There is one with dark, shiny, ochre leaves that we aptly named 'Red Panda', which competes with 'Spotty Dotty', overshadowed by a giant *Podophyllum versipelle* cross over 3 feet tall. Our biggest *P. delavayi*, with bold, black markings and maximum dimensions to its leaves, fills the shadiest spot. *Podophyllum delavayi* really needs moist total shade to be happy. It burns with even a touch of sun, crisping at the edges. Shade here is provided by yet another aralia, tall 'Silver Umbrella'.

Brunnera macrophylla 'Jack Frost' in bloom with *Saxifraga stolonifera* 'Rubra'.

Athyrium niponicum var. *pictum*, more silvered in full shade in moist woodland.

Arisaema consanguineum with silver-centered leaves and *Podophyllum* 'Kaleidoscope'.

> View of the shade border with *Aralia elata* 'Silver Umbrella' by our stand of bamboo.

Acer palmatum 'Geisha' with pink variegated foliage, a beautiful plant but a very slow grower.

Step across the bamboo-lined path and yet another showstopper has taken up happy residence there: *Podophyllum* 'Kaleidoscope'. It is a little drier here, which suits this plant, with striking, dangling red flowers and silver and black markings on its octagonal leaves. What all podophyllums have in common is their love of rich compost and lots of fertilizer. We find that commercial fertilizer leaves burn marks. We prefer something like seabird guano (sustainably harvested), high in nitrogen and only slightly odoriferous.

Varying foliage color as well as texture are especially important to a design in a woodland garden, because here in the shade, flower power happens mostly in a big bang in spring. Unlike yellow, silver colors often become brighter in shadier places. It sounds counterintuitive, but the silver-leaved varieties of painted fern, pulmonarias (such as 'Silvermoon'), and *Brunnera macrophylla* 'Jack Frost', and especially 'Looking Glass', glow more silvery in deeper shade.

We turn a corner to an area with hot morning sun until about 2 p.m. This spot has been a challenge. Hellebores are good for this location: sun or shade, they take it all. More silver-splashed, evergreen foliage on the vigorous, albeit sterile, new hellebore hybrid from England called 'Anna's Red', is a good choice, with its large, red flowers. A small Japanese maple, 'Geisha', with

An area in the morning sun with heucheras giving a strong color accent.

pink- and white-margined leaves, is trying to provide some shade, but it grows so slowly! We have placed the newly introduced, bright heucheras, named frequently after mouthwatering foods and drinks, here and there for color effect. In sun and with adequate moisture, their leaves turn even brighter. Caution is advised: It is easy to get carried away by so many color offerings and, as much as I like boldness, I don't want the border to look like an Easter egg collection. Also, the diminutive Oregon brush rabbits love to eat their foliage. We tone it down with sun-tolerant ferns like the many forms of Alaskan fern (*Polystichum setiferum*) and white astrantias (*Astrantia major*).

Creamy, white-edged foliage of *Eleutherococcus sieboldianus* 'Variegatus' provides afternoon shade. I love this shrub in spite of its somewhat prickly nature. Its gracefully arching branches can reach a spread of 6 feet, with an equal or greater height, but it is easily pruned. A small shrub, *Pieris japonica* 'Flaming Silver', aptly named for its flaming red new growth and silver-edged green foliage, resides at a slight distance from the five-fingered aralia separated by much greenery. A group of shade-tolerant, red *Alstroemeria psittacina* surround the *Eleutherococcus* specimen. Remarkably hardy for a native from Brazil, it has conquered various shady garden spots. We and our hummingbirds value it

for its summer-blooming flowers of green heavily overlaid with red. Next, as we turn on the path, the beds transition into shade again, provided by a magnificent tree, the golden Wych elm (*Ulmus glabra* 'Lutescens').

Many years ago on a trip to Tasmania, in almost every garden, we saw a graceful, yellow-foliaged, large tree, easily the most popular garden tree on the island but unknown in the western United States—that is, until we spied a photo of it in a garden catalog. It was advertised as easily growing 6 feet a year. Because we had just lost a thirty-year-old Douglas fir (one of my very first planted seedlings), which toppled over in a wild rainstorm of hurricane proportions, this elm seemed just the ticket. We needed that shade and fast. A whip arrived by mail and, yes, put on 6 feet the first year, and it seems not to have slowed down much in the following years. It grew so fast that the trunk still kept the slightly arched form of the whip. After the leaves unfold, their golden glow spreads sunshine above, even when the sky is gray. It now spreads filtered shade below. After this one offering in a mail order catalog, this tree has mysteriously disappeared from nurseries (at least in the United States), perhaps because of difficulties shipping elms due to Dutch elm disease.

When our thirty-year-old Douglas fir toppled over into one of the large maples, with its enormous root ball extending vertically in the air with all the understory planting of arisaemas, omphalodes, anemones, and hellebores then

Douglas fir blown over by strong windstorm, exposing root ball.

< Woodland planting backed by *Fothergilla major* and *Acer palmatum* 'Scolopendrifolium'.

Pieris japonica with blue Omphalodes cappadocica at its feet.

Omphalodes cappadocica, and O. cappadocica 'Starry Eyes', which often reverts back to blue.

growing sideways but still intact, we decided to have a crew cut the trunk about 12 feet up. Without the weight of the top of the tree, the root ball settled back into place with a thunderous thud. A large Chinese hydrangea (*Schizophragma hydrangeoides*) vine had climbed the living tree before the toppling, encircling the trunk with its snake-like branches. The 12-foot trunk became the sole support for the vine and turned it from a large dead Douglas fir into a short, verdant schizophragma tree, blooming in midsummer with 12-inch inflorescences of fragrant white blooms under its giant elm tree neighbor. Someday the fir trunk will decay and disintegrate, but a hidden support structure of metal rods will prolong the life of the vine.

Cyclamen hederifolium appropriated the area around the decaying fir trunk, growing thickly with overlapping, silver-patterned leaves. In spring, when the cyclamen foliage deteriorates, the running sensitive fern *Onoclea sensibilis* takes over, then it's thinned in late summer, letting the cyclamen flowers peek through in September. The fern's leaves turn a bronzed yellow in late fall before dying down.

There are a few more shrubs in this woodsy area that have become enduring members of our woodland community. Many others have come and gone, killed by freezes, wet, or drought, or because of the gardeners' displeasure at their aging looks. One of the enduring and endearing, suckering shrubs, *Itea virginica*

> *Ulmus glabra* 'Lutescens' and *Schizophragma hydrangeoides* growing on a dead Douglas fir trunk.

^ *Hydrangea quercifolia* 'Pee Wee' in fall color.
⌃ *Erythronium revolutum* and *Trillium kurabayashii*, both from the Coast Range of Oregon, with *Carex siderostica* 'Variegata'.

^ *Hydrangea quercifolia* 'Snow Giant' in full bloom.
⌃ *Syneilesis palmata* (umbrella plant) and *Fuchsia* 'David'.

'Henrys Garnet', decorates itself with fragrant cream-white pendulous flower racemes in early summer, and brilliant red foliage in fall that lasts all winter into spring until new foliage emerges. These suckers are easy to pull; you just lift the skirt lightly and bottom-prune so there is room underneath its edges for small winter and spring delights such as the silvered leaves of *Cyclamen hederifolium*, snowdrops, and blue corydalis. In our garden, every inch counts. This gardener abhors a vacuum (bare soil).

The front garden path encircles a large bigleaf maple and ends by the driveway. Bigleaf maples are thirsty trees, as everyone knows who has gardened under these large Oregon natives. Even when the soil is covered with a yearly application of compost, their roots meander up to the top within a year. We have learned after many failures what companions will thrive in the root-filled soil under the dense canopy. *Hydrangea quercifolia* is one of the shrubs that lives equally well in sun or shade with little moisture, and is the most drought-tolerant of all hydrangeas. 'Snow Giant' has heads of many-bracted flowers, giving it a double-flowered appearance. Other favorites are a vigorous, upright grower named 'Alice', and two diminutive, slightly contorted varieties, 'Pee Wee' and 'Ruby Slippers'. All have magnificent heads of white, cascading, sterile flowers in late summer and large, deep red, autumnal-toned, oak-like leaves. The color lasts long into winter when other shrubs are barren. We pay close attention to its proper pruning, because flowers are produced only at the end of branches. Vigorous cutting back will produce lots of leaves and no flower show. To keep our most enthusiastic varieties within bounds we head back some branches hard each year to give them several years' undisturbed new growth.

The various shrub-like honeysuckles (*Lonicera nitida* varieties), green, green-yellow, and purple leaved, with their horizontally arching branches, can be grown right at the dry foot of the maple and still be happy and colorful. They are easy to prune into any shape, so they are accommodating and also evergreen. We have never seen flowers or berries on them, perhaps because they are so small. We use *L. nitida* 'Lemon Beauty' with gold-edged, green foliage in this shady spot. Its spreading, horizontal branches can be sheared like boxwood or pruned informally. We lightly shear ours into low, spreading shapes, and they are surrounded by bright yellow-flowered hellebores, *Helleborus* ×hybridus 'Golden Sunrise', with golden spring foliage that turns chartreuse in summer. These are underplanted with golden lamium, the yellow-tipped, low-growing yew (*Taxus cuspidata* 'Nana Aurescens'), and *Epimedium* ×*rubrum*. This epimedium and many other evergreen epimediums grow with minimal amounts of water. Their evergreen foliage is flushed with red in summer and burnished bronze in winter and spring. March flowers appear on 8-inch thin, wiry stems, forever moving with the slightest breeze. We shear all evergreen epimedium foliage back to the ground by late February so we can enjoy the emerging panicles of spurred flowers unobscured by last year's foliage. If sheared later in spring, it is too easy to snip the newly emerging flower stems along with the old leaves. Fresh foliage is soon to follow.

Sadly, our beautiful bigleaf maples have decreased in size over the years. Doubtlessly they would have preferred richer loamy soil instead of the sandy silt that lies beneath our compost. In addition, red-breasted sapsuckers have girdled the tops, killing them. Some years ago, to replace two of the bigleaf maples, we added two dawn redwoods (*Metasequoia glyptostroboides* 'Gold Rush') with golden deciduous needles and fluted trunks, as well as a golden larch (*Pseudolarix amabilis*), which is a pleasant light green in summer, turning golden in fall. You might think, "Too much yellow!" But between the large dark green maples and the backdrop of bamboo, the airy golden needles look light and sunny, turning a rusty color in fall before dropping.

Since the maples, larch, and Chinese redwoods are deciduous, they offer shade in summer and sunlight in winter and early spring for bulbs, hellebores, and ephemeral treasures to thrive. We love the variety of color that covers much of this shady bed for most of the year. Between the epimediums, trilliums, and corydalis, large patches of *Lamium maculatum* 'Beacon Silver', an intensely silver and shade-loving ground cover with dark pink flowers, is allowed to ramble all summer under taller perennials and ferns. We shear it once in summer and pull a bit at escaping edges and remove any green seedlings; they are easy to uproot from the compost-rich soil to keep in bounds. We don't allow them to overrun their neighbors, *Vancouveria chrysantha*, and the tiny, 4-inch *Blechnum penna-marina* subsp. *alpina*, alpine water fern, with coppery, glossy fronds. Many years ago we were given a little piece of the vancouveria, a drought-tolerant, southern Oregon native, a cousin of the epimediums. With diamond-shaped, evergreen leaflets and panicles of starry yellow flowers, it spreads slowly to form a pretty mat tucked in between silver pulmonarias, brunneras, blue-flowered *Omphalodes cappadocica*, and taller ferns. In late winter, we shear the vancouveria once to let fresh spring foliage show to best advantage without the tattered leaves of last year. With such a ground-covering tapestry of leaf and flower abutting each other, growing through and over each other, vying for space, the gardener needs to keep a sharp eye out for overaggressive behavior.

Hakonechloa macra 'All Gold', heucheras, hellebores, and *Lamium maculatum* 'Beacon Silver'.

Trilliums

Wake-robin—what an appealing name, evoking the greening of spring, the first birdsong, and sunlight. I first encountered *Trillium*, an early blooming genus, in the woodland hills of the Oregon coast and the foothills of the Cascade Range. *Trillium ovatum*, cousin of the eastern *Trillium grandiflorum*, never covers acres of ground, but grows more coyly among Douglas fir, spruce, and redwood in isolated patches, offering an entrancing surprise for us spring hikers. For some reason, perhaps climatic, the coastal *Trillium ovatum* can be almost twice the size of its mountain counterpart. The flowers turn a delicate light pink with age.

With my curiosity aroused, I searched for sources of more species. Trilliums are divided into two main groups: pediculate, with flowers borne on a stalk (pedicel) above the leaves, and the sessile group, whose flowers sit directly at the top of the foliage. All trilliums we grow love humus-rich, moist, but not soggy soil in dappled shade. *Trillium ovatum* is a good garden plant for us, coming up about three weeks before the eastern *T. grandiflorum*. Most eastern trilliums come up later than our western natives, so mixing eastern and western species is a good way to prolong the trillium season. Be aware, though, that in our slug- and snail-friendly springs, the eastern species are generally more prone to slug attacks than the western ones.

< *Trillium ovatum* in the garden.

^ *Trillium* 'Ice Crème' in a patch of *Epimedium* ×*versicolor* 'Sulphureum'.

⌃ *Trillium grandiflorum* with blue *Corydalis flexuosa*.

^ *Trillium albidum.*

⌃ Red *Trillium* 'Volcano', a hybrid of *Trillium chloropetalum*.

A case in point is the diminutive *Trillium underwoodii*, with dark red flowers and silver-centered leaves strongly mottled with green and brown. Unarguably it is the winner in "Best Leaf" category. The slugs agree. Even with a ring of blue bait surrounding the plants, they were devoured shortly after unfolding. In its native Alabama and Georgia, it has had no need to evolve with slug resistance. Sadly, we had to give up on this beautiful treasure.

We have hiked the southeastern states in spring among sheets of trilliums, a sight to behold. It seems that most eastern trilliums, even though they do well here, are slower to increase in our gardens than our western species. This quality may be heat or soil related.

Trillium 'Volcano', fiery red in bloom, imposing in stature, and glowing with vibrant color, is an eye-catcher impossible to miss when in bloom or at a plant

^ *Trillium angustipetalum.*

⌃ *Trillium kurabayashii.*

^ *Trillium rivale.*

⌃ *Trillium kurabayashii* with yellow petals, veined red, and very dark, marbled leaves.

sale, where I first encountered it. I absolutely had to have it. We were exhibiting vendors at the sale and allowed to shop early. As soon as the signal was given for the opening of the sale for vendors and volunteers, I fairly streaked through the hall to garner one of these beauties, only available at one vendor stall. To my chagrin, all were already taken—the table was empty. I saw a figure standing close by, cradling *two* pots in his arms. I accosted the man without even taking a look at

his face and rudely asked, "Two!? Why do you need two pots?" A slightly hurt voice answered, "But one is for you." It was a friend of mine, who had rescued one for me. It was a humbling experience.

It was first introduced from tissue culture out of New Zealand. Over years, clumps can take on large dimensions with more than 40 flowers. After some research, we contacted Barry Sligh in New Zealand who had introduced this presumed garden hybrid of

Trillium rivale 'Purple Heart'.

Trillium luteum.

Trillium chloropetalum, a northern California native. He had introduced it through tissue culture, which eventually failed. In the meantime, we acquired all he had and have worked on its production through division ever since.

We also grow a cream-white trillium with a slight hint of pink at the base of the petals, aptly named 'Ice Crème', also selected by Barry Sligh. It resembles the very best examples of *Trillium albidum*, a strong grower with showy white, sessile flowers, well adapted to our gardens. Native to northern California and southern Oregon's Coast Range, it is commonly called giant white wake-robin, or sweet wake-robin.

We have also raised from seed two excellent forms of the western natives *Trillium kurabayashii*, giant purple wake-robin, and *T. angustipetalum*, the narrow-leaved wake-robin. *Trillium kurabayashii* usually has very dark, red, sessile flowers, longer and narrower than *T. chloropetalum*. The foliage in good forms has very dark, almost

black, mottling that will fade with age. Plants are up to 18 inches tall. The leaves can be 7 inches across and the narrow, upright flowers to 4 inches tall. Now and then, yellow-flowered seedlings, veined red at the tips of their petals, appear among the reds with a peculiar but pleasing corkscrew twist to the petals. In 2006 a fellow trillium enthusiast arrived at our nursery with a package of seed of this trillium, collected by him in southern Oregon. It took seven years to flowering from the time first sown, and now we have spread divisions all over shady spots in the garden, mostly because I couldn't bear to part with any of them. I am usually a rather moderate person, but when it comes to collecting beautiful plants, I have the addict's intemperance.

Trillium rivale, from the Siskiyou Mountains in southern Oregon, is one of the tiniest of trilliums in stature but not in flower power. The best form, *T. rivale* 'Purple Heart', has white, purple-centered, spotted flowers growing in a tight cushion. It is covered with flowers in

Trillium cuneatum.

early spring and is the easiest to divide, having longer rhizomes than others that come apart very readily. It must be carefully sited among other diminutive companions or in a shady rockery with good spring moisture.

Elegant red *Trillium erectum*, with lanceolate, almost triangular flower petals, grows for us among pink and blue forget-me-nots fronted by *Blechnum penna-marina* and a glowing turquoise *Corydalis flexuosa* as a final touch. Slow to increase, but with the flowers held for a month in our cool spring, *T. erectum* is well worth trying.

Lost in the annals of our garden history is the year we acquired a tiny start of *Trillium cuneatum*, native to the southeastern United States. Now a good-sized group greets us every March, pushing through a carpet of white *Anemone nemorosa*, and bordered by blue-flowered pulmonarias and *Asarum caudatum*. Our *T. cuneatum* is of relatively short stature, about 10 inches when in bloom, and displays vividly marked, trifoliate leaves shot through with silver on a green background.

An easy spreader, the southeastern, sessile *Trillium luteum*, about 1 foot tall with yellow, erect blooms, sitting on top of nicely mottled foliage, has made its shady home under a Japanese maple in our garden and happily multiplies in a carpet of variegated *Disporum sessile* and low epimediums.

Trilliums, one of our garden's most valued residents, like hellebores, are permanent, reappearing and increasing year after year. They are expensive to buy, and they do require patience. Grown from seed, they take five to seven years to flower, but we have not let that discourage us. Have we not all planted little gallon-sized trees, envisioning sitting under them in the shade many years in the future? At least, when planted from seed, we can have dozens at one time instead of one small treasure. Every year we look forward to more.

across the creek and into the woods

OUR JOURNEY OF discovery takes us across a small vernal creek, adjacent to the driveway, and into another woodland garden. Giant ferns have settled on the steep banks of the little creek and it is hardly visible anymore. The other side of the small bridge used to be our sheep meadow, but the sheep have long since gone and the open meadow changed into a shady grove. Each tree here is a personal friend with a history.

The Douglas firs, planted in the 1970s to screen us from the public road, came from our own forest, transplanted as small seedlings. We had learned through bitter experience that Douglas firs die if transplanted as large specimens. The giant redwood, planted in 1974 and fenced from sheep depredation, has grown into a large tree 3 feet in diameter. The Norway spruce, once bought as a live Christmas tree in a pot, was planted with great ceremony after Christmas right near the house. It soon lost its small conical Christmas tree looks and began to grow and grow, but who can cut down a Christmas tree? A few years later it was moved near the redwood into the sheep meadow with a giant tree spade and tractor.

< The bridge from the driveway into the shade garden.

Arboretum after planting in 1990.

Much later, after the sheep were sold, a portion of the meadow was planted with a mix of deciduous trees and conifers to serve as a backdrop to the garden and to screen it from drying northerly summer winds. We were able to get young trees in small tubes, an affordable way to start an arboretum. We found that small trees generally establish faster and better in a harsh environment like an unwatered meadow. We mulched all the trees, and for two years we used a weed killer to keep their root zone free of grass.

In 1989 we drilled again for more water. The ancient dowser led us to our forest 1000 feet away for our moderately successful second well. Over the years, we drilled more wells—we never take water for granted in our summer-arid climate. The small arboretum across the creek morphed into a shady grove and a large double border, shaded on the south side by a row of Lombardy poplar trees along the driveway, now replaced by aspens since poplars have a limited lifetime here.

With more water available, we were in an expansionist mood. First, brambles and grass had to be killed and the new plot lay fallow for a year. Then we outlined the woodland and long border with undulating, chipped paths and plenty of compost for the beds. We are lucky to live in an area where commercial, well-rotted compost from logging residue and animal manure is readily available.

I love the old-growth forests of our western Cascades, their magnificence, their natural balance, the sensory pleasure I receive walking in them. Certainly I knew I couldn't create an instant woodland like that, but I can observe, learn, and imitate. An old-growth forest is not dark, for example. The lower limbs of conifers have long since died and fallen. Ancient, fallen dead trees or trees downed by storm create islands of light. The recumbent giants slowly decay and serve as nursery beds for new life. Younger and smaller trees like vine maple, hemlock, and dogwood, and shrubs like salmonberry, wild currant, and rhododendron make up the understory. Yearly, a new layer of compost, in the form of needles, lichen, mosses, maple leaves, and animal residues, covers the ground. Hemlock seedlings, evergreen huckleberries, creeping dogwood, twin-flower, ferns, and many small forest residents thrive on well-decayed, barely recognizable, old fallen tree trunks.

Some of this we could imitate. We top-dressed the soil with well-rotted compost, and we limbed up the redwood and spruce for more light. We started planting shade-loving understory trees and shrubs and imported pickup loads of decayed, rotten logs out of our forest, any size we could handle, and all the fungi, microscopic arthropods, bugs, and lots of woodland millipedes with them. We used some of the logs to divide and delineate new beds.

Especially with small plant starts, it is often difficult to envision their proper placement in a large empty bed whose dimensions seem much too

Schizophragma integrifo-lium flowers.

big for the as-yet little plantlets. Placing some well-rotted logs in a somewhat haphazard manner divided the beds into smaller, more visually manageable portions and made placement much easier. The decaying wood will gradually disappear into the compost, adding nutrition. The decayed logs act as a moisture reservoir and a magnet for myriad fern spores, which grow magnificently in that old wood. The adult fern can be easily moved by taking the log, or part of it, with the embedded plant and replanting wherever there is room.

We joined numerous plant societies, both in the states and overseas, all of which in simpler, regulation-free days offered seed exchanges. Ernie loved their seed catalogs and ordered generously each year. Seeds were sprouting by the hundreds in various pots, from rare bulbs and alpines to perennials and

Sequoia sempervirens (coast redwood) planted by Marietta in 1974. This tree and a large *Picea abies* (Norway spruce) dominate this part of the garden.

> View toward the redwood from the bridge.

woodland treasures. It was mostly up to me to find a home for them in the garden. With the addition of the irresistible purchases from plant sales and specialty growers, we could have filled those new beds in no time. But instead of impulsive planting in a helter-skelter way, we started with the anchoring plants, the understory trees and shrubs that give structure to a new garden. Dogwoods (*Cornus* spp.) and Japanese maples thrive in part shade and gave us that layered canopy so pleasing in a woodland.

Understory trees and shrubs need to provide more than a short season of interest for us. Besides early bloom, *Cornus mas* offers bright red berries in fall, and the variegated form lightens the shade with its cream-edged leaves, as does the large *Stachyurus* 'Magpie' in a dark corner under the redwood. We use quite a bit of variegated foliage in the shade. As long as there are ample rich green tones to complement the many variegations, it becomes a harmonious whole and the eye never tires looking at the richness of Nature's endless variety.

Soft swaths of *Hakonechloa macra* 'Aureola' lining the path invite the garden traveler into this magic woodland. Even though this part of the garden is adjacent to our country road it feels like entering a painting by Rousseau. Could there be some wild thing hiding among those giant Asian mayapples, skunk cabbages, rodgersias, and royal ferns, or behind the giant rice-paper trees (*Tetrapanax papyrifer* 'Steroidal Giant')? All large tree trunks are veined with twisted, knotty vines of schizophragma, *Hydrangea anomala* 'Miranda' or *Eleagnus pungens*, both 'Maculata' and a silver-leaved form.

Some of our favorite small understory trees and shrubs include: *Acer japonica* 'Aconitifolium'; *A. palmatum* 'Osakazuki'; camellia, good in dark shade and drought-tolerant, such as *C.* ×*williamsii* 'Donation' (light pink), *C. japonica* 'April Remembered' (soft pink), or *C.* 'Pink Icicle' (blush pink); *C. alternifolia* 'Argentea'; *C. kousa* 'Summer Fun'; *C. mas* 'Variegata'; *C.* 'Venus'; daphne, also drought-tolerant, such as *D.* ×*transatlantica*

Trollius chinensis 'Golden Queen'.

Convallaria majalis 'Hardwick Hall' and *Phegopteris decursive-pinnata*.

'Eternal Fragrance', *D. odora*, and *D. tangutica; Enkianthus campanulatus;* rhododendrons with silvered and cinnamon new growth, such as *Rhododendron* 'Golfer' with silver tomentum or *R. pachysanthum* with brown felty indumentum; *Calycanthus ×raulstonii* 'Hartlage Wine'; *Stachyurus* 'Magpie'; *Styrax obassia;* and *Tetrapanax papyrifer* 'Steroidal Giant'.

We use three variegated forms of spreading lily-of-the-valley, *Convallaria majalis* 'Striata', with yellow-green striped leaves, 'Fernwood Golden Slippers', a rich golden form, and a dark green, yellow-edged form that seems to be offered under a variety of names, 'Hardwick Hall' among them. This variety makes a balanced twosome with the creeping Japanese beech fern (*Phegopteris decursive-pinnata*), neither overpowering the other. The white flowers of the lily-of-the-valley make the quintessential Mother's Day bouquet, with the most powerful delicious perfume. In my childhood, we used to have our secret sites in the beech forests of Germany like truffle hunters do here in the coniferous forests. The competition was intense to bring a fragrant bouquet of the wild Maiglöckchen (little May bells) home to the delight of adults and was a victory for the bearer.

Evergreen ginger (*Asarum europaeum*) with shiny foliage, five-finger fern (*Adiantum aleuticum*), hellebores, silver lamiums, and epimediums leave no ground exposed. A shady rockery and patches of *Adiantum venustum*, a drought-tolerant evergreen maidenhair fern from the mountains of Asia, surround the Norway spruce, whose roots spread far and wide in search of water.

The rockery is the home of plant treasures of smaller stature, like *Anemonella thalictroides* f. *rosea* 'Oscar Schoaf', with pink pom-pom flowers, and hepaticas, with silver-marbled leaves and early season blue and pink flowers. We raised the area slightly with extra rock and wheelbarrows of soil to give our relatively flat landscape a bit more contour to show off the smaller plants. We added a few slow-growing small shrubs to give some height variance without swamping the plants beneath.

Trillium rivale, low, late-flowering woodland saxifragas, hardy orchids, and the short, almost black-flowered *Arisaema sazensoo* cannot compete with the hulking neighbors in adjacent beds. A bit of oakfern (*Gymnocarpium dryopteris*), a small creeping epimedium (*Epimedium ecalcaratum*), yellow-flowered with spiny red foliage in spring, and a very small form of *Anemone nemorosa* with blue-centered white bracts, are about all the competition these plants can handle.

Convallaria majalis 'Striata'.

We use chipped paths, which become an ideal growing medium as the chips age. Who knew about the slumbering capabilities of the once rare and expensive Asian mayapples? Years after initial planting, in ideal soil conditions, their growth becomes exuberant and the territory beyond the path is just more acreage to conquer. The more I dig, the more they grow. Each cut end of an underground stolon produces a new plantlet.

I love the multicolored jungle on the moist side of the redwood. Podophyllums like dark, shady places. They do well in competition with other plants, mostly by killing them since their leaves make such a dark canopy. But fast, tall, upright plants such as the variegated *Fatsia japonica* and tree-like *Tetrapanax papyrifer* 'Steroidal Giant' with its enormous leaves can win the battle for light. Tall *Disporum cantoniense* and the 6-foot, deep red–flowered *Polygonatum kingianum* also grow above the massive mayapple foliage. The tendril-tipped leaves of the Asian Solomon's seal clasp a Japanese maple to keep from falling into the massive sea of leaves below. This lovely polygonatum deserves much greater popularity.

On the opposite side of the bed, where the Douglas fir roots meet the redwood, perpetual drought resides. We can water and mulch as much as possible but the trees' roots swallow it all. Fortunately, though, there are shrubs

that live well under these conditions. Evergreen *Camellia japonica* is surprisingly drought-resistant and offers additional screening from the road. For this dark area, we selected soft pink–flowered cultivars like *C. japonica* 'Donation', 'April Remembered', and 'Pink Icicle'. Drought-loving, evergreen *Daphne odora* adds fragrance. *Calycanthus ×raulstonii* 'Hartlage Wine', a vigorous grower even in dryish shade, glows red, covered in bloom all summer long and then tops it off with bright, butter-yellow fall foliage.

Another evergreen drought lover, *Elaeagnus pungens* 'Maculata', the silverthorn or thorny olive (produces no olives), has morphed from a large shrub with gold-streaked foliage into an even larger vine, hugging the trunks of the forty-year-old Douglas firs. Some of its variegated leaves have reverted to silvery green, also quite handsome. We have not pruned those reversions out since they hang from high up in the firs.

Stachyurus 'Magpie', with attractive white-margined leaves and drooping racemes of early flowers, thrives here with tree root competition. We planted several *Mahonia ×media* 'Arthur Menzies' along the outskirts of the trees, tough plants in any environment, with the hope that their prickly foliage would deter

Anemone nemorosa 'Bracteata' sport with *Epimedium ecalcaratum*. A sport is a part of a plant that shows morphological differences from the rest of the plant. Sports may differ by foliage shape or color, flowers, or branch structure. In other words, it is a mutation of a growing root or branch tip.

^ *Calycanthus* ×*raulstonii* 'Hartlage Wine'.

⚹ *Epimedium* 'Amber Queen' and *Disporum sessile* 'Variegatum'.

^*Mahonia* ×*media* 'Arthur Menzies'.

⚹ Epimedium in a carpet of maidenhair fern, *Adiantum venustum*.

^ *Geranium* 'Anne Thomson'.

⚹ Podophyllums, *Polygonatum kingianum*, and *Cornus alternifolia* 'Golden Shadows'.

sneaky deer invaders in midsummer, while their yellow flower sprays in late fall delight us and our winter-resident Anna's hummingbirds. Acting as backdrop among the mahonias, deciduous *Ilex verticillata* 'Winter Red', another large drought-adapted shrub, drapes cascading branches covered in bright red berries over the lower greenery. A small male among its lower branches assures us of a heavy fruit-set.

Ferns of all varieties, such as shield ferns (*Polystichum* spp.), buckler ferns (*Dryopteris* spp.), painted fern (*Athyrium niponicum* var. *pictum*), Himalayan maidenhair (*Adiantum venustum*), and even the magnificent, enormous royal fern (*Osmunda regalis*) grow well in the acidic, drier soil near the conifers, in spite of their supposed preference for moister conditions. In late winter and very early spring, snowdrops and trout lilies carpet the ground here, followed by masses of blue and white woodland anemones and *Omphalodes cappadocica*,

Bench in woodland underneath *Hydrangea paniculata* and *Ilex verticillata* 'Winter Red'.

with forget-me-not-blue flowers. Other perennials, such as the many cobra lilies, pushing through the earth a little later, can easily penetrate these low early spring messengers. It is like a parade of color and form, constantly changing, layering, and overshadowing each other, delighting and surprising us with the changes throughout the seasons. In late winter, when most of the verdant leafy growth retreats underground, we cut back ferns and epimediums and enrich the soil with another layer of aged compost.

the long shady border

WHEN WE FIRST conceived the idea of a long border divided by a path through the center, we thought of somewhat emulating the idea of an English border often glorified in garden magazines. Our desire was to create a less controlled, more naturalistic, version. The somewhat crescent-shaped path was to be 4 feet wide, but Nature has literally encroached upon that idea over the years. The two-sided border now is 125 feet long and of varying width, from 15 to 30 feet.

We determined right at the start (1989) that the north half of the border, to the south of our fledgling arboretum, was to be a shrub and tree border, mainly to limit our expansionist tendencies. To here, but no farther! We also hoped that dense shrubbery taken together with two alert greyhounds would deter the deer somewhat from encroaching in summer. And here was a chance to plant more trees.

Chamaecyparis lawsoniana 'Elegantissima', clothing itself with cream-colored, nodding branch tips each spring is a truly elegant conifer, tall and narrow, a selection of an Oregon native tree. The two Oriental spruces, *Picea orientalis* 'Skylands', were an outstanding ornamental success. The trees now have grown to a 30-foot height. Deep yellow fan-like sprays of new growth cover them throughout the year.

< The long shady border looking west to 'Esk Sunset' maple (*Acer pseudoplatanus* 'Esk Sunset') and Norway spruce (*Picea abies*).

Bo, the friendly greyhound deer deterrent.

> Weeping giant redwood (*Sequoiadendron giganteum* 'Pendula'), its bark riddled with hundreds of sapsucker holes.

In spring, thousands of red male strobili (mini pollen cones) adorn the trees. It looks like the conifer has broken out in bloom. "What, a flowering spruce?" astonished visitors exclaim.

We designed a careful selection of smaller deciduous trees to complement the conifers. When a design is planned by a professional on paper, one imagines the mature result appearing within the year, which almost never happens. It usually takes several years, and with us it took much trial and error, before a "final" result materialized. Some trees that had looked wonderful in catalogs or nursery containers didn't thrive and died in our weather and soil conditions. For the various mountain ash trees we planted, the soil was too acidic and too wet in winter. Redbud (*Cercis canadensis*), katsura (*Cercidiphyllum japonicum*), and various snake-bark maples were all subject to verticillium wilt, a soil fungus that causes branch die-back and usually eventual death. Then we watched with dismay as the many beautiful but destructive red-breasted sapsuckers devastated many young trees. They have an unpredictable predilection for certain trees, the weeping *Sequoiadendron giganteum* being their all-time favorite, but flame ash (*Fraxinus oxycarpa*) is a close second, and there are many more. A sapsucker can

Cornus 'Venus' (a hybrid dogwood: *Cornus kousa* 'Chinensis' × *Cornus nuttalii* 'Goldspot' × *Cornus kousa* 'Rosea').

actually girdle a young tree to the point of death with many puncture wounds, all seeping the sweet sap that he so much likes to sip.

But let's talk about the successes. The various dogwoods have grown beautifully. *Cornus alternifolia* 'Argentea', multi-stemmed with white-margined leaves, loves the light shade the conifers provide. Variegated *Cornus kousa* 'Summer Fun', *Cornus mas* 'Variegata', and *Cornus* 'Venus', the latter with enormous pure white bracts, as well as the profusely flowered *Cornus kousa* 'Milky Way', are beautiful in all seasons. The leaves on the variegated forms are pleasing to the eye and not strident. All bear red fruit and colorful leaves in autumn. We prefer *Cornus kousa* or kousa hybrids over the similar, early flowered *Cornus florida*, which has a predisposition to anthracnose, an ugly and destructive leaf fungus, sometimes even killing the affected tree.

A more recent discovery has been the graceful genus *Styrax*, with very fragrant white or pink-tinged, bell-shaped flowers. Since they are a woodland genus, they also flourish in the half-shaded border, both *Styrax obassia* and the new variety *Styrax japonicus* 'Evening Light', with dark purple-black foliage. The white bellflowers contrast wonderfully with the dark leaves.

Styrax japonicus 'Evening Light'.

Clematis 'Westerplatte' and *Sambucus nigra* f. *porphyrophylla* 'Black Lace'.

To hopefully make this garden an impenetrable deer deterrent thicket, we sprinkled shrubs between the conifers and deciduous trees. Small and sparse looking at first, it has now become the thicket we had hoped. It has kept us from enlarging the garden further, at least in the northward direction. We did find ways to break our "no more plants" promise in other ways, though, by going south and planting more densely.

I have learned not to plant conifers densely together, be it shrub or tree form, as whole branches die with lack of light and cannot be pruned back after needles have dropped, with the exception of yews, which are very shade tolerant. The shrubbery of the dense, north-facing border was planted in leafy, competition-tolerant plants only. There is such a wealth of beautiful combinations and choices, but it was important to us to include multiple season interest.

I am an intense and intensive gardener. The wealth of variety in form, texture, and color the natural world provides is immense and delightful to the senses. A blue sky every day becomes too much of a good thing, but add a few clouds, a puff of wind, a shower now and then, a change of light, and magic happens. There is an awakening, and so with plants. Harmony and contrast, or one may call it harmonious contrast, alerts all of our senses. The silver-felted leaves with brown indumentum of *Rhododendron bureavii* × *R. smirnovii* interspersed with the purple lace of *Sambucus nigra* f. *porphyrophylla* 'Black Lace', the white flowers of 'Sally Holmes' rose, and sprays of pink elderberry flowers satisfy the visual senses. Fragrance and bird songs, hummingbirds and bumblebees buzzing make our garden a paradise.

Our planting choices run to single specimens or in threes, sometimes twos. When a plant is a special favorite, we will grow it in more than one garden area or intersperse it repeatedly among others along a path, providing continuity, as we did along this walk with the densely flowered snowball *Viburnum plicatum* f. *plicatum* 'Pink Sensation'. It sports dark-tinged, pleated foliage and arches gracefully toward its shrubby neighbors. Large shrubs, *Rosa glauca*, blue-foliaged and pink-flowered, and a giant, fragrant mock orange (*Philadelphus* hybrid) clad in May and June with snow-white double flowers, its name having become lost to us now, provide the backdrop. The highpoint of a large mock orange lies in those fragrant, white flowers in spring. It is of minor interest the rest of the year, but makes a great green background plant since its size can be well over 8 feet. I find it best unpruned except for cleaning out the deadwood inside, and since the legs on an older plant can be somewhat bare, it is clothed with the borrowed dress of smaller shrubs. Ours is fronted by a summer-flowering *Hydrangea paniculata* 'White Moth', also large, with enormous panicles of pure white sterile flowers. (To keep *Hydrangea paniculata* within bounds without losing the yearly show of those grand flowers, prune last year's flowering twigs down to one or two nodes. Two new flowering branches will grow from each node at the end of the branch. At the same time, take out any dead wood.) The legs of *H. paniculata* 'White Moth', in turn, are shod with the low-growing layered *H. quercifolia* 'Pee Wee'. These three shrubs are hedged in on one side by variegated *Cornus mas* and on the other side by purple-leaved *Physocarpus opulifolius* 'Diabolo'. We want the garden to delight our visitors and ourselves, not just through the abundance of flowers, but with myriad combinations of texture, shape, and color of foliage alone, so that the garden is of interest throughout all seasons.

Along the border, clematis and sturdy perennials snake their way between the shrubs, giving the impression of a colorful wall, impenetrable but friendly. This keeps the visitor directed along the path. To invite occasional meditation and rest, we have placed benches and chairs in strategic places in the garden, in hidden, private spots or in areas that offer a particularly good view. A bench backed by a trellis covered with the fragrant rose 'Westerland' divides this long, shrubby border in the middle, and not only visitors but even we will sit now and then to look at the ever-changing flower border across the path and enjoy the fruits of our labor.

After we had rototilled and composted the part of the meadow that became our north border and planted the trees and shrubs facing the north side of

Long border path flanked by *Viburnum plicatum* f. *plicatum* 'Pink Sensation'.

Hydrangea paniculata 'White Moth' with *Clematis* 'Purpurea Plena Elegans'.

Fragrant, climbing *Rosa* 'Westerland'.

Primula sieboldii at the front of the border can tolerate much dryer conditions than most primulas.

Rodgersia pinnata 'Bronze Peacock'.

the path, we were confronted by the very long (125-foot), empty bed on the south side, ready to become the English border of our dreams—a somewhat intimidating prospect. How do you start? The perennials of our choice came in small 4-inch or at most gallon-size pots, looking forlorn in that large emptiness. I sat on the bench that commanded the view of barrenness and envisioned the future abundance. It helped to place sticks and flags, and even each other with wide-spread arms, at strategic spots visualizing future shrubs and trees as permanent structural elements.

In a new large planting, many of us gardeners tend to place the little plantlets much too closely since they look so forlorn and small. To avoid that, I spent time researching the speed of growth and eventual height and width of our new acquisitions. Now, twenty-six years later, a good part of that border lies in semi-shade. The trees and little shrubs have spread their limbs and leaves. There were failures also. Insect damage and verticillium wilt took their toll. We learn to accept Nature's unpredictable ways.

To exclude the view of the driveway from the path through the long border, on the north side of our tiny vernal creek we planted a shrubby visual barrier. *Hydrangea arborescens* 'Annabel', deutzias, *Cotinus coggygria* 'Royal Purple', *Rosa moyesii* 'Geranium', *Cornus alba* 'Kesselringii', and best and biggest of all, *Eleutherococcus sieboldianus* 'Variegatus', have proven to be very permanent and showy back-of-the-border residents. Fronting the wetter end of the border is a colorful mix of candelabra primulas in various orange and red tones, together with big chestnut-leaved rodgersias (*Rodgersia aesculifolia*), which

< The border in late spring with *Eleutherocuccus sieboldianus* 'Variegatus' and blooming rodgersias.

'Esk Sunset' maple (*Acer pseudoplatanus* 'Esk Sunset').

> *Fallopia japonica* 'Variegata' with almost completely white leaves.

are a bit on the thuggish side but controllable by yearly spade pruning of their rhizomes.

The primulas sulked a bit in June, wilting from too much sun. A chance to plant a new tree! A new Norway maple from New Zealand had just been introduced, *Acer pseudoplatanus* f. *variegatum* 'Esk Sunset'. Ernie and I had a bit of a disagreement about that one. It is a maple with strong, pink-cream and green stencil markings on its foliage, which he saw as resembling spider mite damage, but I saw the future, namely the deep copper-red color on the underside of the leaves, and I envisioned myself looking up into that reddish glow. Every morning now, only a few years later, as the sun alights on the tree from the east, it glows with a coppery sheen, reflected also in the dark purple smoke tree below and the red flowers of a *Rosa moyesii* 'Geranium'. It is a daily morning light show we watch with enchantment, and the primulas, now joined by blue corydalis (*Corydalis flexuosa* hybrids), are happier in the afternoon shade.

Going eastward along the border the colors change abruptly to metallic purple and almost black tones with *Allium christophii* and *Actaea simplex* 'Black Negligee' interspersed with the darkest black-red–flowered *Lilium* 'Night

^ *Hydrangea macrophylla* 'Sandra'.

⌃ *Rhododendron pachysanthum*.

⌃ *Astrantia major* 'Ruby Wedding'.

^ Hybrid martagon lily 'Claude Shride'.

⌃ *Rhododendron* 'Golfer', with spring foliage.

⌃ The lily *Cardiocrinum giganteum*.

^ *Hibiscus syriacus* 'Red Heart'.

⌃ *Lilium lankongense*, a fragrant, shade-loving lily that spreads gently by rhizomes.

⌃ Long-flowering *Clematis* 'Hagley Hybrid' keeps its color in partial shade.

Flyer' leaning into them like a friendly neighbor. The black grouping ends with a very dark-leaved dahlia with flowers of white and purple tones.

Now, back to sunshiny yellow. Nobody can accuse me of being subtle. I love the stark contrast of almost black tones intermingled with yellow, but this combination must be used sparingly. Too much of it and the eye and mind grow weary, like watching too many thrillers.

The yellow-variegated five-finger aralia (*Eleutherococcus sieboldianus* 'Variegatus'), a shrub that grows to 8 feet or more, is fronted by my favorite hardy fuchsia, 'Genii', its yellow leaves brightest in the sun and totally free of leaf scorch. The red tubular flowers are loved by hummingbirds. With enough moisture, even the weeping, 2-foot-high Bowles' golden sedge (*Carex elata* 'Aurea') thrives in full sun, looking its golden best. The border continues in a filtered mix of sun and shade created by two *Acer griseum* and a dark-leaved, pretty-in-pink crabapple, bearing the somewhat pompous name *Malus* 'Royal Raindrops'. Thalictrums, asters, astilbes, pulmonarias, and even giant cardiocrinum lilies, live in harmony under one of our oldest residents, *Fallopia japonica* 'Variegata'. Knowledgeable gardeners abhor *Fallopia japonica* (commonly known as Japanese knotweed) because of the decidedly over-aggressive tendencies of its creeping rhizomes. The variegated form, clad in ghostly white foliage with only the tiniest splatter of green, is emphatically less aggressive, at least in the Pacific Northwest. Each shoot, protected from the sun by the Royal Raindrops crabapple, grows to about 8 feet. I am surprised they grow at all with so little chlorophyll in their leaves. The rhizomes have not strayed from their allotted space in fifteen years. If a shoot arises in a spot already occupied by another plant, it is easy to pull it with a twitch of a hand. Late summer panicles of cream, funnel-shaped flower clusters enhance their beauty.

Maturity and age have mellowed my biases and opinions. Even in the theme of landscape design, our prejudices, early acquired, can blind us to much that could be beautiful when thoughtfully incorporated in a planting. The strident, jumbled, color mismatches of our local rhododendron gardens in spring had turned me off the whole genus, but I now use many of the rhody gems, as I did in this border in the shade, primarily for foliage effect but for a good flower show too.

Early rhododendron breeders selected for ever-bigger and gaudier flower trusses, a trend that does continue into the present, but recently many breeders consider outstanding foliage of prime importance. Superior choices for this border include *Rhododendron* 'Golfer', with silver tomentum on the new leaves that lasts all season, *R. pachysanthum,* with cinnamon-brown felted leaves, and *R.* 'Sir Charles Lemon', with copper-red tomentum as well as young stems of a reddish color. I also chose a *R. bureavii* hybrid for its furry brown leaves and stems. Lastly *R. bureavii* ×*yakushimanum*, combining the brown and silver foliage of both its parents, looks elegant with *Corydalis flexuosa* weaving through the felted leaves. Most of these carefully chosen species and hybrids clothe themselves in white to light pink flowers, not overabundantly or outstandingly gorgeous, but still giving a pleasing effect. Flowers are of short duration, but good foliage is an asset lasting all year long. The leaves, we believe, are the more important feature of a rhododendron.

Moving east on this long border, late-blooming trumpet lilies, fragrant turkscap, *Lilium lankongense*, and hydrangeas mingle with bergenias, astilbes, and astrantias at their feet. The lilies give us much desired scent and bloom later in summer. A vigorous, bold comfrey, *Symphytum ×uplandicum* 'Axminster Gold', with variegated leaves a good 2 feet long, lights up the eastern end. We use an easy touch in this border so different now from its original intention. Self-sown aruncus, red astrantias, and even the twining vines of *Dicentra scandens* are watched but not eradicated. Sometimes Nature is a better designer than any of us.

The border ends with an eye-catching effect of the very dark foliage and pink flowers of *Rodgersia pinnata* 'Bronze Peacock', repeated in the black-tinted leaves of *Hydrangea macrophylla* 'Sandra'. The large white sterile florets of these lacecap hydrangeas are suffused with a band of red at the edges, looking like groupings of little butterflies ready to take wing with the next breeze. These hydrangeas are my absolute favorites. They stop me in my tracks whenever I pass by. Dark red turkscap lilies, *Lilium martagon* 'Claude Shride', grow happily amid the hydrangeas in light shade.

A small bridge under a canopy of blue and white *Wisteria sinensis* leads from the long border to our driveway. In late winter and early spring we would continue past the bridge to the end of the garden along a large bed of selected forms of *Helleborus ×hybridus*, used here as the sole perennial under a red-twigged selection of vine maple (*Acer circinatum* 'Pacific Fire'), a Chinese dogwood (*Cornus kousa* var. *chinensis* 'Milky Way'), and a winter hazel (*Corylopsis spicata*). The quiet, evergreen summer ground cover bursts into glorious, eye-popping colors each February and March and lasts well into April. If this were happening in June, we would be less impressed, being satiated with color all around, but with the continually gray Pacific Coast skies of late winter, this jumble of bright colors delights and satisfies.

In our early gardening days we grew pink *Geranium ×oxonianum*. If you have one, you will soon have a thousand and more, so all our plants were thrown as compost into the unirrigated meadow adjacent to this part of the garden. Undeterred, they multiplied and we found that the deer loved them. As soon as the deer can mow them down they grow back, and this has worked well for us, since the entrance into the garden just past the geraniums is all hellebores, absolutely distasteful to deer. We like to think that the delicious explosion of geraniums helps to keep the deer from exploring farther, except for the rare adventurous one now and then.

> The wisteria-covered bridge leading to and from the long shady border.

Arisaemas

The hooded flowers of arisaemas bring mystery to a woodland garden. Their Jack-in-the-pulpit flowers are actually colorful spathes, hiding rather insignificant flowers inside on the spadix. The plants produce either female or male flowers. Fat and well-nourished plants will likely be female, having enough vigor to produce seeds. With their energy spent, the next year they may revert to being male, producing only pollen. The "Jack," or spadix, is in the "pulpit," or spathe. The true flowers are arranged on the lower half of the spadix, hidden within the tube, a clever arrangement that serves to trap the buzzing insects within, at least long enough to either pollinate the female flowers or to cover itself with male pollen to then hopefully travel on to entrap itself in a female flower.

In fall, we find those decorative red fruit spikes among the dying arisaema foliage as a cluster of berries, each containing one to ten viable seeds, which will usually sprout in early spring of the next year. Ernie discovered a clever trick to make sure of seed production should the insects fail us in the case of particularly beautiful plants, such as *Arisaema sikokianum* with its silver-centered foliage. With a turkey baster full of water and a small yogurt container, he goes from plant to plant, male and female alike. You never can be exactly sure of the sex from year to year without invasive examination, risking damage to the flower. He squirts water down the tube, catching it with the yogurt cup at the bottom of the spathe tube slit, and repeats the process with the same water from plant to plant. In this way he spreads watery pollen from male to female.

< *Arisaema sikokianum* with silver-centered leaves.

89

Arisaema serratum with silver-centered leaves.

Arisaema taiwanense fruiting spike.

Arisaema sikokianum, from Japan, well known and loved by woodland connoisseurs, arises early in spring. Its inflorescence, with a dark striped spathe, white inside, fairly glows, encircling the white club-shaped spadix, the whole looking a bit like a bewitched ice cream cone. We are very fond of forms with variegated foliage, usually with a silvery pattern along the midrib of its trifoliate leaves. In moist, leafy, but not soggy, soil, it will reappear for years. It does not seem to make offsets, so seed propagation is the way to go. Start with at least two or three plants to ensure that both sexes are present, and only harvest seed when it is red and ripe and germinates well.

Originally we received *Arisaema takedae* (or ×*takedae*) seed from Ontario, Canada. *Arisaema takedae* has puzzlingly been put into *A. serratum*. This hybrid with *A. sikokianum* (*A. sikokianum* ×*takedae*) generally has a darker spathe and a lighter and larger spadix and sets seed prolifically. With an abundance of silver-leaved seedlings three years later, we were able to plant lavish groupings in appropriate woodland spots and ascertain its hybrid origin. We learned that sunlight scorches their

leaves. Under the dense shade of aralia and a weeping bald cypress, among companions of paris, low ferns, and epimediums, these vigorous plants with inflorescences almost as beautiful as *A. sikokianum* and bright silver-centered leaves grow bolder and bigger each year.

Under the protective shade of the bald cypress, *Arisaema costatum* unfolds its giant, tripartite leaves with showy red midribs and margins. Dark maroon spathes, with white stripes and deeply curved hoods ending in a long tail, huddle together well below the foliage. The inside of their inflorescence is lit up by the white stripes, misleading pollinating insects that mistake it for an exit. Bouncing off its walls, insects linger a bit longer, increasing the chances of pollination.

From here our magical mystery tour leads us to *Arisaema griffithii*, a cobra lily that truly has the look of its namesake but without the deadly bite. The low, wide-eared spathe, yellowish on the outside, colors to dark, mottled maroon on the curled inside, with a long, thin tail (appendage) leading downward. This shape is designed to entice an insect to its entrance via pheromones on the appendage. Very decorative trifoliate

Arisaema costatum.

Arisaema candidissimum.

leaves with reddish margins lure the garden visitor to inspect more closely. For us, the plants go down each year by midsummer, but the springtime drama makes up for the early dormancy.

Arisaema ringens, with two shiny trifoliate leaves, also emerges early in spring, but lives on until rain or frost in fall drives it underground into winter rest. Our plants have never produced seed, but the short, 8-inch, flowering stems with tightly curled, dark spathes, are pretty to look at. The plants are wider than tall and their glossy leaflets show up well, surrounded by lacy, creeping Adiantum venustum ferns (Himalayan maidenhair).

Similar in leaf but not in flower, late arising Chinese Arisaema candidissimum, meaning the "most white," is indeed that. It is the only arisaema with a white spathe striped pink on the inside. Its very showy blooms open in early summer for us, prolonging the arisaema flowering season. Digging some of its numerous offshoots from around the main tuber and planting them separately is the fastest way to propagate new plants. Do this during dormancy. Arisaema candidissimum is an easy plant to grow, doing equally well in our woodland

at the foot of a tall Norway spruce, or among ferns under moister conditions.

We are members of an online group called Arisaema-L, which in addition to having many knowledgeable members with whom to discuss proper identification, also has a seed exchange. We have received many choice seeds of species and varieties not found easily elsewhere. One of these was a diminutive, very dark form of the Japanese Arisaema sazensoo. The leaves superficially resemble a small A. sikokianum. The spathes, with nearly black hoods, only reveal their internal white stripes and the bulbous, white spadix on close inspection. Planted among the short ground covers of yellow Epimedium ecalcaratum and white-bracted Anemone nemorosa, they present a real focal point in our shady rockery.

The long-necked giraffe among arisaemas, with a darkly mottled petiole, is Arisaema nepenthoides, over 5 feet tall. It is worth growing just for its size and oddness. A spotted, mottled flower sits atop the long, skinny petiole. Plant it in a protected spot away from wind, or near shrubbery that it can lean on.

Arisaema sazensoo.

Two more arisaemas are worth mentioning here. Both have radially symmetrical leaves like spokes on a wheel (technically palmate). *Arisaema taiwanense* pushes through the ground with its leaf looking like a folded umbrella, which then opens into 11 to 15 radial leaflets on a purple and green mottled petiole about 2 feet tall and almost as wide. It is quite a sight. The reddish brown, striped inflorescence grows underneath its leafy umbrella. We have seen enormous, thick fruits so low and heavy that they touch the ground when ripening to a rich red in late fall. The plants can be propagated by seed or also small offset tubers, which they produce prolifically at the top of the main tuber. *Arisaema taiwanense* was brought into cultivation just recently in the 1990s. After initial doubts as to their hardiness, I was surprised when they survived −10°F (under 10 inches of snow). Strangely, the silver-leaved form of this species was devoured by meadow voles that left the green form untouched. I have tried to grow it several times, but finally gave up because it was expensive buying more specimens, only to have them disappear once again.

The easiest of all arisaemas that we grow (with the exception of the overly vigorous *Arisaema ciliatum* var. *liubaense*) is also one of the best. *Arisaema consanguineum* is the latest to appear, only breaking dormancy in early July for us. When summer slows the exuberance of spring, then it is the time for *A. consanguineum* to rise above grasses, ferns, and hellebores to dance like many thin-legged spiders on narrow swaying pseudostems. We have, over the years, selected leaf forms with the most silvered and narrow leaflets, often with long elegant drip tips.

They enliven the summer woodland with movement and color. Each year I find more spots for them to lighten up dull corners. Their inflorescences are narrow,

Arisaema consanguineum silver, in front of *Cornus mas* 'Variegata'.

Arisaema ciliatum var. *liubaense*.

mostly purple with paler stripes. Their highly decorative fruits turn downward when red and ripe to lay themselves onto yellow grasses or dark green ferns. They are the last arisaema slipping into dormancy, going down only with the first frost.

If voles are not a concern, *Arisaema thunbergii* subsp. *urashima*, with long spadix appendages like fishing lines, is an easygoing and showy species, having glossy leaves and purple and white spathes. Sadly, I find only gaping holes wherever I planted them. The same goes for tall *A. tortuosum*, with its dark mottled stems and upright, curved spadix appendages. They look as if they are thumbing their nose at the world and so, it seems, the voles took umbrage and ate every one of them.

Only one arisaema, of the many we have grown over the years, I cannot recommend— *Arisaema ciliatum* var. *liubaense*—since it spreads by stolons to create an arisaema jungle, leaving shorter plants underneath in summer-long darkness. It also spreads by seed. Its flower and look are very similar to a green-leaved *A. consanguineum*, but its stoloniferous, vigorous habit is not. So I pull it out each year, hoping to curb its vigor.

No woodland garden should be without arisaemas. They add a primeval touch to the garden, with their intriguing flowers, their often silver-mottled leaves, and bright red fruit. Some almost look sinister, some humorous, some downright beautiful. And all add an element very different from any other flowering plant I know.

Arisaema amurense.

musings from the kitchen window

ACROSS FROM THE bigleaf maple bed, where forty-five years ago a white picket fence, now long gone, led from the road past the house, we come to our "kitchen view bed." It is shaded by the north side of our two-story farmhouse and by a large Mount Fuji flowering cherry tree, with horizontal branches spreading 40 feet wide. In April, the tree is covered with a snowstorm of white semi-double flowers. I planted it in 1973 as a fragile stick with spindly arms, little imagining how wide it would spread and how many shrubs and ground covers would thrive under its umbrella.

Our large kitchen window faces this bed looking north. How pleasant it is, watching birds and flowers when washing the dishes. Suet cakes, sunflower feeders, and hummingbird feeders hang from cherry branches and the sturdy climbing wisteria vine by the window. Bird book and binoculars are within reach of soapy hands. The Mount Fuji cherry (*Prunus* 'Shirotae') has become a social center for the birds. The clownish looking acorn woodpecker, with its bright red cap, is the undisputed king, his sharp beak commanding respect even from the larger, bossy Steller's jays. Nuthatches, chickadees, and juncos are winter residents, joined later by red-winged blackbirds with their liquid voices, and big, clumsy, band-tailed pigeons, goldfinches,

< Mount Fuji cherry (*Prunus* 'Shirotae') and *Rhododendron pseudochrysanthum*.

Evening grosbeaks at the feeder.

and many more. The messy jay hacks at the suet while smart spotted towhees, doves, and finches scurry on the ground, pecking at the manna that drops from the feeders. And the hummingbirds zoom and dive, competing for their sugar water source.

Now and then, the harmony is disrupted by a sharp-shinned or Cooper's hawk striking like a lightning bolt from a hidden perch. In a flurry of panic, all birdlife disappears. Sometimes a lone feather drifts slowly to the ground, evidence of a sudden death. And, just a few minutes later, harmony is re-established.

I meditate on the difference between bird and man and look at the brilliant, white hellebores in my view field. It is early spring. That large grouping of white hellebores glows as darkness sets in at dusk, and it will light up again in the early morning. We named the strain, quite appropriately, Sparkling Diamond. It took many years of hand-pollinating and selecting to develop the pure white, double flowers that now bloom below our window.

Over the many years we have lived here, both the kitchen window and the view have grown grander. Twice the window has been enlarged and the view has grown from driveway, meadow with sheep, and distant road to

^ The old homestead in the early 1970s with a white picket fence surrounding it.
⌃ View from the kitchen window in summer.

Wisteria and bird feeder from another kitchen window.

The view from the window, featuring *Cornus kousa*, *Cotinus coggygria* 'Royal Purple', and *Rosa* 'Geranium'.

an ever-changing, engaging garden scene with a backdrop of trees planted over years. The view of the road has been obscured by a giant green curtain of distant 65-foot Leland cypresses (*Cupressus × leylandii*). The driveway itself is flanked by a row of aspens. They have been limbed up, exposing the white trunks topped by leaves shimmering in the breeze, and so deserving of their name, quaking aspen. In fall, they turn to gold as if with by a Midas touch.

The aspens are a beautiful asset as well as a curse in a garden. A large grove of aspens in the wild may all be a single clone, spreading over millennia, the age of the stand being more than ten times older than a single ancient bristlecone pine. The quaking aspen, an American tree (*Populus tremuloides*), and its relative, the European aspen (*Populus tremula*) are by nature stoloniferous and continue this habit in the garden, throwing up root sprouts twenty feet, or more, from the mother plant. These shoots grow seemingly overnight. For us, the aspens' beauty outweighs this annoyance.

Across the driveway from the white hellebores, at the foot of the aspens, drifts of white daffodils bring brightness to our often gray spring days. White-blooming

Cyclamen hederifolium leaf forms.

spiraeas serve as a backdrop leading to the woodland across our creek. In late summer, fall, and winter, masses of silver-hued *Cyclamen hederifolium* cover the ground in this summer-dry bed lining the driveway. The daffodils grow up in March, just as the cyclamens go dormant but then reappear in August—a timely exchange. Dark blue, bearded iris will follow the daffodils. They love the aspens' root-bound, dry soil. Also at this time in late winter, between the aspens, two Cornelian cherries glow with thousands of tiny, deep yellow clusters of flowers. Behind my perch at the window I can't even smell their pungent odor of wet dog. This must be the reason for the whole genus name of dogwood, even though all the other species are quite inoffensive. But, again, beauty outweighs the downside and in fall the dogwood merits its other name, Cornelian cherry, bearing bright red, edible fruit, albeit very sour.

Creating a complex planting in this kitchen window bed with some visual appeal for most, or all, of the year was important. Looking out at an ever-changing scene throughout the year, I realize how lucky I am. No high-rises, roads, or suburban views for me, but instead a green paradise. I recently took an inventory

Smilacina racemosa.

A very dark-leaved form of *Trillium kurabayashii*.

Rhododendron 'Laramie'.

Carex elata 'Knightshayes' with *Podophyllum* 'Spotty Dotty'.

of the plants that jostle for attention in this bed and was amazed at the numbers that manage to co-exist (with stern supervision, of course). *Rhododendron* 'Laramie' with fat buds like miniature artichokes and fuzzy indumentum-covered leaves borders the driveway under the old Fuji cherry, accompanied by trilliums and our native *Smilacina racemosa* topped by sweet-smelling white plumes. In March, little pink tongues push out of the artichoke buds and they develop into glorious white flowers. The east side of this bed is bordered by *R. pseudochrysanthum*, densely packed with blush-pink flowers turning white with age in April. Dense foliage and a tight structure are a bonus. The tedious and sticky job of removing the spent flower remains and pruning and thinning is lovingly done by Ernie in May. Rhododendrons lightly pruned right after flowering will form new flower buds for the next year. The same is true for daphnes, but daphnes are usually headed back rather than thinned.

The purple-foliaged Japanese maple 'Trompenburg' overshadows the bed, reaching toward the cherry. The hydrangeas in the center of the bed, scented *Hydrangea angustipetala* 'MonLong Shou' and *H. macrophylla* 'Lady in Red', are pruned to 40 inches in height, keeping our view open. A well-mannered riot of form and color (a contradiction in terms, but nonetheless possible) grows beneath and around the shrubs from April into fall. Covering the soil at the lowest level are robust pink-flowered *Dicentra formosa*, needing a lot of shovel control, evergreen *Asarum caudatum* with semiglossy leaves only 3 inches tall, and silver-mottled *A. splendens*. I recommend the various asarum species highly for gardeners who garden in dense and even dry shade.

From March through May the graceful *Anemone nemorosa* reigns as the supreme ground cover in this bed. It grows well in shade or sun as long as the soil is loose and rich. Under the Mount Fuji cherry, white and blue forms abound, going dormant at the end of spring. March and April are the flowering time for our native pink and white fawn lilies (*Erythronium* spp.), with their spotted foliage appearing early enough to beat the crowd of bigger plants that could inhibit their bloom. After buying the first expensive plants of these spring charmers, Ernie collected fresh seed wherever he could find it (*E. revolutum* is a native of our Coast Range), including among the flowering plants in our garden, and scattered it throughout the woodland garden. It was a most successful enterprise. Now, his hand-sown seedlings light up many of the shaded areas of the garden in early spring with their cheerful, nodding pink blossoms.

An all-red mix of *Trillium sulcatum*, T. *recurvatum*, black-red T. *kurabayashii*, and the highly appreciated wine-red T. 'Volcano' share space with newly rising red astilbes, variegated Solomon's seal, epimediums, and our beautiful, irrepressible *Corydalis flexuosa/elata* hybrids in turquoise, blue, and purple. As the white hellebores fade to soft green, the magic of podophyllums takes over my view from the window. We enjoy playing with the repetition of big and bold leaves. Podophyllum leaves recur in all of our shady moist beds in endless variation of color patterns and heights, slowly growing into large clumps. To increase their spread more quickly we dig around them lightly with a spade to sever their rhizomatous roots. Each cut will sprout a new mayapple shoot. Lots of organic fertilizer helps, too.

Japanese forest grass (*Hakonechloa macra* 'Aureola') is overlaid in late summer and fall with strands of the red-flowered *Tropaeolum speciosum*, a nasturtium relative from South America. We have combined it with the bronze autumn fern (*Dryopteris autumnalis*) at the edges of the bed to soften the long, straight border. The latest to bloom are the sweet-smelling, white, bottlebrush flowers of several crowns of *Actaea matsumurae* 'White Pearl'. Situated in the middle of the bed, they tower above even the hydrangeas. In early summer, we place gridded supports above them, which become invisible in fall. In November and early December, I watch the acrobatics of finches and towhees dangling on the tips of their pendulous branches to eat the delicious seed. We never tidy up for winter here until all the seeds are gone.

> *Tropaeolum speciosum.*

Favorite Spring Bulbs, Corms, Tubers, and Rhizomes

A year is just long enough to be surprised again and again by almost forgotten, often ephemeral, bulbs, corms, tubers, and rhizomes that slumber underground. Because ephemerals are here and gone so quickly, they can be grown in the same space as later emerging perennials that enlarge to share their space.

In our garden, all the more permanent ground covers are selected for their ability to share space with seasonal flowers. In the Pacific Northwest, winter and spring rains are a given; maybe for a short time a thin white blanket of snow covers the earth—a rare occurrence in our valley. Mostly, the skies are gray, and only the omnipresent Douglas firs give a relief of green. But, not so around our house. Late in January and February the garden comes alive, alive from the ground up. Slowly, the tightly curled buds of hellebores unfold. Bright, very bright, yellow-flowered hellebores, the result of years of breeding, are the first to light up the shady borders surrounding the house, the first emerging perennial.

They are accompanied by ever-increasing crowds of snowdrops, but not just ordinary snowdrops, even though those also abound. In 2003, on a February trip to England, Ernie was bitten by the galanthophile bug

< *Galanthus* ×*valentinei*.

Snowdrops (*Galanthus nivalis*) and apricot-yellow hellebores.

Galanthus elwesii, unnamed selection.

Galanthus ×valentinei.

Cyclamen coum.

and has been buying expensive little gems ever since. It must be contagious because, after initial resistance, I succumbed. From short and tubby to long-stemmed, elegant white, often with unusual green markings, they dance in the wind, undisturbed by our daily showers and occasional freeze. The various species and varieties hybridize in gardens, and beautiful, large-flowered selections can be had for greater or smaller pocketbooks. Our favorites are the large, round-flowered varieties such as *Galanthus* 'S. Arnott', robust 'John Gray', and stately 'Seagull'.

Frothy masses of pink *Cyclamen coum* blossoms spring up seemingly overnight from buds hiding under round, silver-mottled foliage that had unfurled in October. The cyclamens are only 4 inches tall but carry a lot of flower power, blooming profusely from January to March. Little goblets of bright yellow *Eranthis hyemalis* flower between the snowdrops. You can order winter aconite (*E. hyemalis*) tubers from catalogs but they usually arrive dead, because they don't survive dry storage well. It is better to buy a potted 4-inch flowering plant. They set seed in great quantities, so we have sprinkled fresh seed in much of the garden over the years, beginning with the two that originally came up out of a hundred bought and, year by year, have been rewarded by ever-increasing patches.

Another very small and very early tuber, *Corydalis solida*, mostly from eastern European meadows and woodlands, deserves much more popularity. It is easy to grow and very colorful, with racemes of light purple, white, pink, and even red flowers (*C. solida* subsp. *solida* 'George Baker'). Best in the rock garden or little troughs because of its short stature, it reappears year after year and increases by seed and tuber offsets. We grow ours right outside the back door in companionship with a group of *Cyclamen coum*, our early spring heralds.

The technical differences among bulbs, tubers, corms, and rhizomes are not very useful distinctions for the gardener. The differences are often confusing to the nonbotanist. The plants possessing one or the other structure could perhaps best be called geophytes. They all use an underground storage structure of some sort to aid in surviving a period of conditions undesirable for growth, like winter or a dry summer.

Eranthis hyemalis in black mondo grass (*Ophiopogon planiscapus* 'Nigrescens').

In our woodland and perennial beds, later covered with taller shade plants and summer flowers as yet dormant, grow carpets of *Chionodoxa luciliae*, also known as glory of the snow. Multitudes of 4- to 5-inch-tall, starry-eyed flowers, most with white centers, crowd many beds, cheerfully facing rain and even snow. Over time, the early acquired various species have hybridized. Some are white centered, some all blue. We found the pink form 'Pink Giant' to be too coarse and leafy, providing only about a week of perfection before slowly and ungracefully declining.

Drifts of the tiny, deep-yellow *Narcissus cyclamineus*, only 6 inches tall with long, thin trumpets, are also claiming more territory in the front of the border. The petals, or perianth segments, like those of its namesake, cyclamen, are bent back toward the stem, giving it a windblown look even in the mildest weather. Short, deep blue *Scilla siberica* is an ideal companion.

Narcissus cyclamineus, being from moist, alpine meadows in northwest Spain and Portugal, dies in dry storage so is never seen in bulb catalogs. It is, therefore, best grown from seed in a grower's flat. It takes about four years to flower but the reward is great, especially so early in the year. It is our only narcissus to bloom reliably early together with the snowdrops and is of a similar stature. We planted it successfully in winter sunny sites in well-composted beds, often mixed with blue *Chionodoxa luciliae*, another early bloomer.

> *Corydalis solida,* in pink and purple tones, and *Santolina virens* 'Lemon Fizz'.

Narcissus cyclamineus and *Scilla siberica.*

Erythronium revolutum (pink) and *E. multi-scapoideum* (pale cream).

Erythronium revolutum, a native of our coastal mountains, is a most attractive and easygoing bulbous spring charmer (it's actually a corm). It carries one to three violet-pink, pendant flowers per stem, and I love their deeply mottled, broad foliage. They are usually only available at plant sales as potted starts, but do not despair. Freshly sown seed will produce many more. Don't weed those little grass-like blades coming up around the flowering mother plant a year later. The year after that, the first true leaf will appear, and after two more years, the seedlings will flower. We usually harvest fresh seed from all our erythroniums and scatter them in suitable areas—moist, acid, humus-rich woodland soil. Be careful when trying to transplant older plants. The bulbs pull themselves deeper into the soil each year.

Other freely flowering fawn lilies scattered about our woodlands include the bright yellow, tall, *Erythronium tuolumnense*, with green foliage, the white, brown-centered *E. californicum,* E. *citrinum,* and E. *multiscapideum,* and the many hybrids of each. For some reason, hybrids, such as yellow 'Kondo', 'Pagoda', 'Citronella', and, best of all, 'White Beauty', are easier to find in catalogs than the species. Erythroniums are also known as dogtooth violets, since their pointed, curved corms really resemble a white canine fang. We prefer their other, prettier, names, such as fawn lily or trout lily, after the spots on the leaves of many species. But under any name, this spring flower is delightful among low ferns such as oak fern, or among the red blades of *Blechnum penna-marina,* or with blue corydalis. Wherever they seed themselves, they are welcome.

The loose compost we spread each year and the pieces of rotten logs from the forest we place in woodland beds have encouraged an exuberant growth of mosses, at their best and greenest in winter. Carpets of mosses, together with the emerging lacy foliage of our spreading, blue-flowered *Corydalis flexuosa* and *C. elata* hybrids, green up the shady borders in March. That early in the year, the corydalis is still a low carpet that does not yet outcompete small bulbs. Later on, it provides a good foil, hiding the fading snowdrop and winter aconite foliage.

We think back on how our fondness for corydalis started in the early '90s when we were given a precious

Erythronium 'Pagoda' with *Corydalis flexuosa* hybrid.

Ipheion uniflorum 'Alba'.

offering from China, a little piece of a new, blue corydalis (then unidentified, but later established to be *Corydalis flexuosa*), soon named 'Blue Panda', which was growing in the garden of a friend. We planted it into our sunny rockery, exactly the wrong site. It languished until we learned of its preference for moist, rich soil. Slowly, many blue and purple C. flexuosa forms came onto the market, and also an early summer-blooming species, C. elata. Over the years, the two hybridized and gave us ever more colorful forms. Then, one year a mysterious explosion happened. They were everywhere, outcompeting smaller ground covers. It covers many beds in spring in glorious blues, and is easy to cut down when it is done in early summer.

You always know when you accidentally bruise the narrow linear leaves of *Ipheion uniflorum*. They exude a powerful smell of onions. But, aside from that, the selection is a charming, easygoing spring bulb when planted in a sunny, summer dry spot. Native to Uruguay and Argentina, it is well adapted to our northern climate. The best and most diminutive form, at 4 to 5 inches, is *I. uniflorum* 'Rolf Fiedler'. The leaves are

topped with true blue, open flowers with white centers. There is also a pure white form, *I. uniflorum* 'Alba', quite showy and about 6 inches tall.

Anemone nemorosa is a woodland carpeter from Europe, spreading by stick-like rhizomes just below the surface of the soil. It covers our woodland beds enthusiastically with leaf and flower in spring. By early summer, it has gone back underground to slumber until the next spring. I came upon this entrancing plant at first during childhood in the wilder areas of the park in Corvey Castle. Knowing nothing about it but smitten, I moved a clump into my own little garden plot. As *Anemone nemorosa* does not rise above 3 to 6 inches in height, other spring bloomers can grow with it or through it.

The open, up-facing anemone flowers come in shades of blue, white, and pink. The single blue forms, 'Allenii' and 'Robinsoniana', and the single whites, 'Lychette' or 'Wilks' Giant', are the fastest and most popular varieties. The pink-flowered variety, 'Rosea', performs a magical act of transformation, opening white, then turning a dark pink when mature. 'Vestal',

Anemone nemorosa 'Viridiflora'.

a pure, double white with orderly, symmetrically arranged tepals, is an old variety known since 1870. It starts to bloom in April, the latest and smallest of all, increasing slowly, but is considered by many to also be the most beautiful.

Another form, 'Bracteata', has single white tepals surrounded by a ruff of green, white-flecked bracts as an ornamental collar to the central bloom. One spring we spied a much-improved mutation among a drift. The central flower, now apetalous, had surrounded itself with large, white bracts, shading to blue in the center. Even larger bracts, green with white variegation, surrounded the former. All in all, it had the look of an extra-large, lacy white, blue-centered flower that bloomed on and on until the whole plant went dormant in June. The flower itself was an illusion since the colorful bracts (actually a modification of leaves) took its place. As eager gardeners, we isolated this marvel and now grow it among black-hooded, short *Arisaema sazensoo*.

More diminutive, at 4 inches tall, *Anemone ranunculoides* is clothed in bright yellow blooms, while its hybrid with *Anemone nemorosa*, *A. ×lipsiensis,* carries flowers of cream-yellow. Again, these rhizomatous anemones are best bought as plants since the brittle rhizomes do not survive dry storage. It is easiest to beg a dormant piece, or even a clump, from a generous gardener. It can be divided into short pieces and laid horizontally in the ground only an inch deep. It will spread faster in loose soil with compost mulch.

Ficaria verna 'Brazen Hussy', as its name implies, is a striking plant found in a hedgerow by great plantsman Christopher Lloyd in his garden in East Sussex. Having black leaves and brilliant, buttercup-yellow flowers, brazen is not an overstatement. It multiplies but is short in stature, and slips into dormancy by April. We enjoy it under deciduous trees, a situation still sunny in March and later covered with large trilliums and epimediums as the trees leaf out. Watch out for green-leaved seedling reversions back to the straight species; they should be pulled with their axillary bulbils. They are not as pretty and can overwhelm the cultivars. There are several double varieties with demure flowers of cream or yellow like small pom-poms, such as 'Bowles's Double' or 'Double Mud'. All these will go dormant by April.

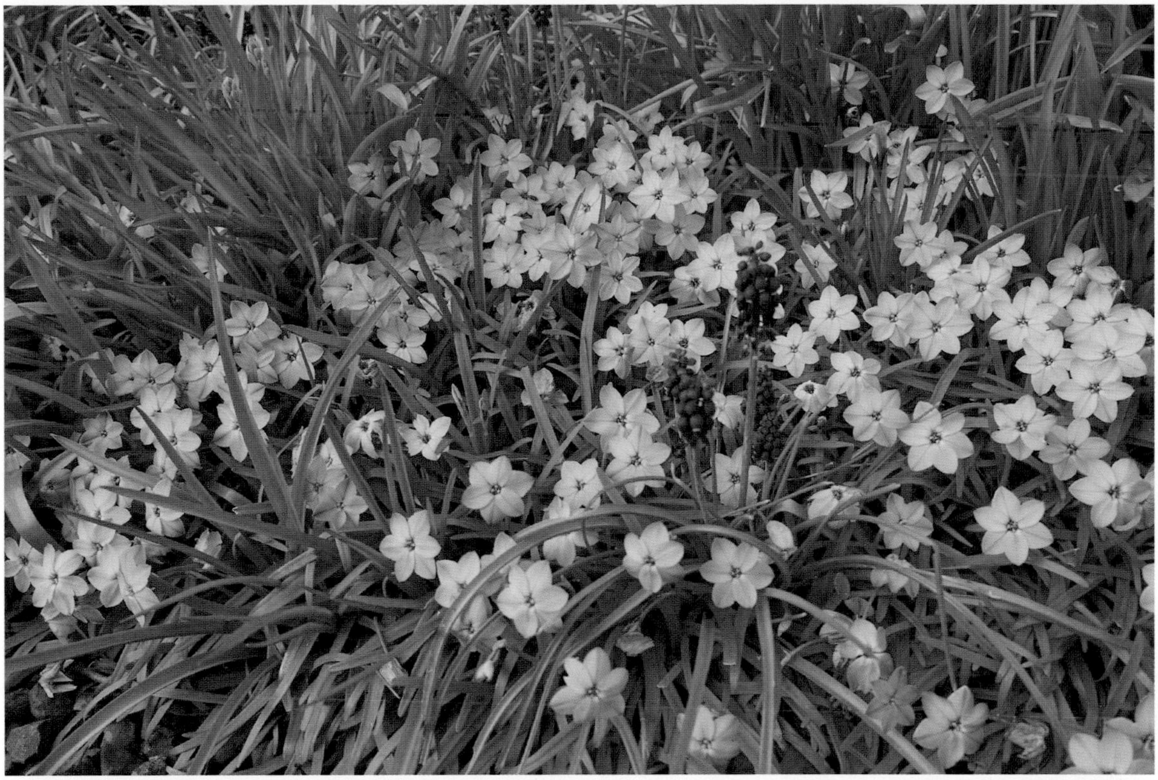

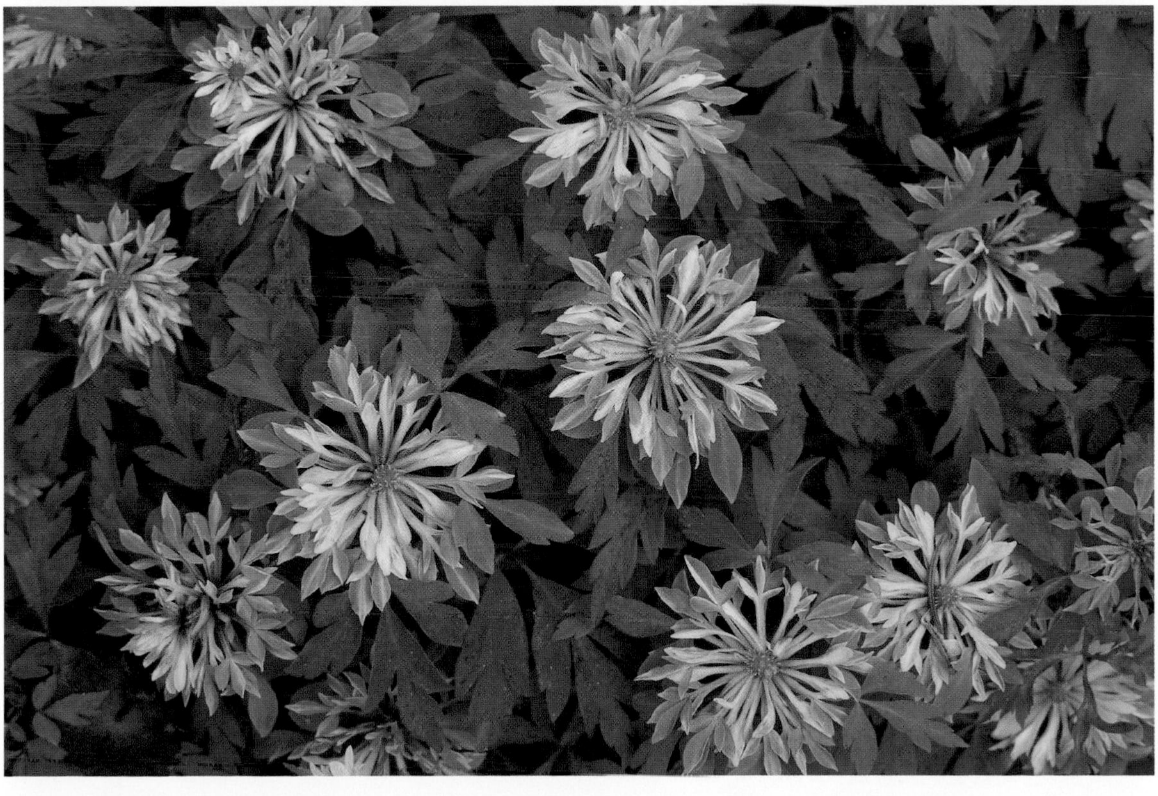

^ *Anemone nemorosa* 'Bracteata' sport.

^^ *Ipheion* 'Rolf Fiedler'.

life around the goldfish pond

TURNING THE CORNER from the kitchen window on the shady north side of the house, we come to sunnier aspects on the northeast side. To screen the garden from the driveway we planted a mixture of shrubs and conifers. A Japanese pine (*Pinus thunbergii*), pruned yearly to give it a broad, layered look, is underplanted with purple flowered, scented February daphne (*Daphne mezereum*). Japanese pines take well to pruning and shaping and can easily be kept to a height of 12 feet. A 6-foot *Abelia mosanensis*, with arching stems and fragrant blooms, drapes itself over hellebores and pachysandras. The abelia, in turn, is overshadowed by our fast-growing, elegant, native western hemlock (*Tsuga heterophylla*). I have always loved the fresh, light green of new spring growth and the graceful, lax branching habit of hemlocks. They appreciate some moisture. A garden setting suits them well. *Rhododendron* 'Virginia Richards', planted over thirty years ago from a gallon pot, covers its 8-foot frame with flowers of an intriguing apricot-pink in May. In summer, *Clematis* 'Étoile Rose' climbs over and through the rhododendron's southern half to keep the sun from scorching its leaves, with only partial success. One day, slow *Stewartia malacodendron* will more successfully shade it completely.

< The goldfish pond.

Candelabra primulas and Japanese iris at the wet seeps on the edge of the pond.

We planned a rockery and barbecue pit that would be screened on the south side from the driveway. What put the idea of a barbecue pit into our heads, I do not remember. It turned into a short-lived project. We dug a rectangular pit down to three feet in the center and banked up gradually at the edges. But then, before we had completed our plans, in the supermarket checkout line I skimmed through the newest garden magazine, and there it was: a small water lily pond, alive with goldfish and water lilies, edged with moisture-loving grasses, ferns, and flowers. It was an instant recognition—here was the real reason we had been digging that giant hole.

The unfinished barbecue pit became a pond. If plants and soil come right to waters' edge, the water is wicked up and needs replenishing. We wanted the

Pacific tree frog.

pond to appear to be a natural part of the garden, lined with boulders and plants growing on and over the edge, so we needed to have a trickle of water constantly flowing into it. We connected a hose attached to a valve so we could control the flow—well hidden, of course, by some boulders. Our pond, even though a small one, brings so much life into the garden.

In spite of full sun, orange candelabra primulas and Japanese irises, with sword-like leaves and blue-veined flowers, thrive here. Ferns and carex grass line the north side of the pond with an overhanging prostrate hemlock, giving the fish a bit of shade in summer. Little, double-flowered marsh marigolds (*Caltha palustris* 'Flore Pleno') dips right into the water's edge, with yellow pom-pom flowers in mid-spring.

The big bullfrog we named Jabba the Hutt.

One of many garter snakes residing near the pond.

Goldfish and koi live in their watery element amongst the greenery. A little fountain splashes and aerates the water. Birds and dragonflies come to visit, the former to bathe and drink, the latter to hunt, mate, and lay their eggs. Bullfrogs come, then colorful garter snakes that can swallow a bullfrog many times their girth. Newts float up to the watery surface to take a breath now and then, and the pads of the water lilies serve as landing stations to countless thirsty insects. In summer, a small paved area by the pond under a red shade umbrella is our favorite breakfast spot.

One day Jabba the Hutt appeared, with a huge mouth, bulging eyes, big flabby belly, and a gray-black back. He is an enormous bullfrog that resides in summer at the bottom of the pond with occasional outings to a rock on the edge and during winter sleeps in the filter system surrounded by bubbly oxygen-rich water. He is not a dumb frog. We assume he goes on nightly hunting excursions in summer. In winter he is stoic and can be held by any child. Our Pacific tree frogs and their pollywogs live by the very noisy hundreds in the raised irrigation tank, into which the bullfrog cannot climb. There they are safe from predation until they mature and enter the garden when they may become food for the garter snake and the bullfrog. The latter two in turn may become food for a kestrel and the coyote from the meadows. There is drama in a garden.

< Waterlilies in the pond.

the rockeries and alpine troughs

THERE WAS A time in our idealistic and enthusiastic youth when we considered building an alpine garden decorated with all the most difficult treasures displayed in rock garden society journals. We joined the local Rock Garden Society, visited Siskiyou Rare Plant Nursery, a treasure trove of alpines in the much drier regions of southern Oregon, and went to work. We built small mountains, hauled stone, spread gravel, and built troughs for the tiniest alpines, all in an effort to imitate in a small way our favorite places in the mountains. The mounds east and south of the house became studded with the gems of the alpine world, and they grew, at least for a time. We started many from seed sent by alpine garden societies from all over the world.

What we didn't consider was that our Pacific Northwest climate was unlike montane regions such as Colorado. We are blessed with a moderate climate—dry summers that these plants liked, but come winter the giant Pacific Ocean sends fog and rain and very moist air instead of snow and intermittent sunshine. We live in the bottom of a valley not at heights of the Cascade Mountains. Fungus and mold attacked our most cherished alpines, and they languished and longed for their home under snow and ice.

< Rockery view with *Armeria maritima* 'Rubrifolia', *Scleranthus biflorus*, sempervivums, and mugo pine.

> Building the rockeries in 1985 with the old swimming pool/irrigation reservoir hidden by a trellis fence.

The same view of the rockeries many years later.

For winter rain protection, we cut little Plexiglas roofs and mounted them on metal rods for many of the most sensitive, but the alpine garden looked in winter like a discarded greenhouse project and the moist air alone brought blackspot and rot, even in extremely well-drained soil. If we could bring a rare and difficult plant to flower and take a photo before it succumbed, we considered it a success.

Not anymore. We learned to be satisfied with plants that thrive in our climate and soil without endless fussing and plastic roofs over their heads in winter. The mounds have become places for tough alpines and small perennials, and, dare I say it, even lowly annuals. The area is screened from the driveway to the north by large conifers and shrubs.

Our main entry is on the east side of the house, facing away from the country road. From here, we go through some of the rockery beds to the garage, or to do our daily chores, may it be nursery, garden, farm, or chickens. Only first-time visitors use the "official" front door facing the road. The alpine mounds now accompany us through the year with a varying tapestry of small trees, shrubs, and low-growing flowers. Our entrance is designed to give a warm welcome to the house and garden beyond. In late winter, when much of Nature still slumbers, small bulbs and corms are pushing through the earth together with our favorite tough perennials, the hellebores.

Both *Cyclamen coum* and *C. hederifolium* are invaluable here as winter ground cover for their foliage alone. No two plants alike, we have selected many plants with an array of shapes and patterning, from silver-marbled to solid silver forms. They are easy to grow from seed and will even seed themselves slowly but surely, making a sizable patch. *Cyclamen coum*, with rounded leaves, cheerfully blooms in January and February in pink, purple, or white through our coldest days, even through the occasional snowfall or heavy freeze. *Cyclamen hederifolium* will bloom in August-September after arising from summer dormancy, its foliage going dormant in April. Both are wonderfully paired with bright yellow winter aconite (*Eranthis hyemalis*) and snowdrops (*Galanthus* spp.).

In March the rockery is strewn with blue and white starry flowers of the diminutive *Chionodoxa luciliae*, an easy reseeder, and with our treasured, tiny *Narcissus cyclamineus*. We grow more each year from fresh seed. Hardy survivors, many species of dwarf conifers were planted at the beginning of our rock garden venture and are pruned yearly to conserve their dwarf and sculptured appearance. Even a dwarf form, if given time and left to its own devices, will grow to considerable proportions unsuitable for a rock garden. The shaped conifers stand as solid sentinels over a constantly varying mass of bloom and leaf in summertime and add solid and interesting structure in winter, especially important because we look directly onto many of the rockery beds from our bedroom windows.

Cyclamen hederifolium.

Cyclamen coum.

Chamaecyparis obtusa 'Crippsii', with bright yellow tips and upright conical growth, has been kept to a height and width of 6 by 4 feet by Ernie's faithful yearly winter thinning and shortening of its scale-like needles. Left unpruned it would be three times that size at least. We take pride in our charges, and Ernie would not forgo this yearly ritual. Behind the Hinoki cypress, a group of three cone-shaped, pruned boxwoods repeat the formal pattern.

Dwarf larches, hemlocks, mugo pines, and miniature hollies comingle with short herbaceous perennials. The deep purple, narrowly upright Japanese maple, 'Twombley's Red Sentinel', serves as backdrop to *Eucomis comosa* 'Sparkling Burgundy', of the same color, with purple-red *Allium spherocephalum* and, for contrast, yellow *Tanacetum vulgare* 'Isla Gold' cavorting among them. Loose meets stiff and harmony is established. Plants jostle each other and embrace—salvias, penstemons, geraniums, sedums, violas, lilies, Cape fuchsias (*Phygelius* spp.), the list goes on. The smallest, such as saxifrages, dianthus, pink scutellarias, helianthemums, and the low, creeping *Daphne cneorum* var. *verlotii*, covered in spring with pink, fragrant flowers, front the beds so as not to be overwhelmed by larger plants.

The eye and senses fatigue with too much sameness—too much small foliage, too much of the same color, too many even heights. Along the rockeries we planted a few small Japanese maples, which would not outgrow their space and could be pruned and thinned into desired shapes. *Acer palmatum* 'Mikawayatsubusa', naturally contorted and spreading horizontally, is ideal as a shady

Variegated tradescantia (*Commelina communis* 'Petit Jean') and *Eucomis* 'Dark Star'.

Acer palmatum 'Mikawa-yatsubusa'.

umbrella for the more sun-sensitive companions beneath. *Polypodium*, ×*Mukgenia* (think *Mukdenia* × *Bergenia*), and the hellebores, 'Pippa's Purple' and 'Winter Moonbeam', both with silver-marbled leaves, thrive here. *Acer palmatum* 'Shishigashira', with branches stretching skyward, each clothed in densely packed tiny leaves, would be comfortable even in a very small garden since it stays narrow and upright but is improved by pruning and thinning.

Every plant in our garden has a story to tell. The oldest member of the "small" trees, forming the upper layer of the garden by the back door entrance, was (and is no more) a *Laburnum* ×*watereri* 'Vossii', a golden chain tree. At its feet we planted a very small pot of a newly acquired exotic vine called *Hydrangea anomala* subsp. *petiolaris* var. *cordifolia* 'Brookside Littleleaf'. We purchased this plant at the Rock Garden Society meeting in 1984 in Bellevue, Washington, from an exciting small nursery vendor called Heronswood, which since then has become legend and history. When the laburnum died, the hydrangea took the place of the tree, its gnarly, multiple trunks now supported by hidden iron rods, and it is still living, with a bit of pruning now and then. The bed underneath has become shadier over the years and the plant palette slowly changed with it. What used to be a bed of sun-loving cushions has been replaced for early bloom with small shade-lovers like *Thalictrum ichangense* 'Evening Star', mossy saxifrages, *Corydalis flexuosa* hybrids, dactylorhizas, and hellebores. Eucomis, collected from seed in South Africa, ferns, and blue *Platycodon grandiflorus* 'Sentimental Blue' only 6 to 12 inches tall, enjoy partial shade as well. Small epimediums provide a ground cover. The weeping *Carex oshimensis* 'Everillo' is definitely a bright gold, loving the shade, and since I adore purple and gold together, how could I not choose the almost black-leaved, tiny mounds of *Rhododendron* 'Everred' as contrast. The back of the leaves of this small treasure are as black as soot, and to top it off, its bell flowers in spring are the dark red color of ripe dark cherries.

A dark, purple-black, dwarf *Geranium pratense* 'Midnight Reiter' sowed itself between the two 'Everred' rhododendrons, creating a designer triangle. Also self-sown are several *Digitalis ferruginea*, blooming in July with rusty blooms on tall skinny stems, one stem supporting a lily this year in seeming cooperation. I would never have thought to design these combinations. Our only contribution was not to weed too precipitously and to exercise restraint. Leave yourself the option to say, "Why not?" We don't practice strict designer principles in our gardens, opting instead for an informal and natural look.

In midsummer, purple-rose *Allium cernuum* and *A. carinatum* subsp. *pulchellum* push their way up through the jumble of flowers, self-sowing, easily controllable, beautiful and underused. *Allium carinatum* subsp. *pulchellum* also comes in a white-flowered form, which is equally pleasing. Their elegant flowerheads take on shapes of fountains of fireworks, with falling sprays of individual flowers in unequal lengths, the complete plant being only 18 inches tall.

Eastern U.S. native *Clematis viorna*, with dainty bell-shaped flowers, has hybridized with *Clematis texensis*, a vivid red-bloomed species of equally diminutive stature. *Clematis texensis* pined for a more alkaline environment and departed eventually but left numerous hybrid offspring. These hybrids are so small they can cavort among the alliums and salvias without smothering them. Their dainty bells drape themselves over and between other flowers like decorative Christmas tree chains. In shrubs they will climb until they reach a sunny spot to dangle and cling, draped with their bellflowers all summer. Their seed heads, silky recurved umbels that eventually turn fluffy, can be left on their hosts all winter, even after the plant itself has slipped into dormancy. They are easy to tend and rarely seen in gardens. If you buy *Clematis viorna* or one of its hybrids in a container, it looks small, thin, and insignificant. Don't let that deter you. They are tough and long-lived, returning from the ground year after year to decorate perennials and shrubs. And they can be easily grown from seed.

From the back entrance of the house, we can take a gravel path to the south, arriving at a large patio. Time to rest, eat, meditate, and host guests. Come in, stay a bit, be at home. You are welcome here. That's what a bench, a chair, any seating, says to visitor and resident alike. This is a place of refuge. All over the garden we have offered seating possibilities. In truth, being work-obsessive, I rarely use the seating in the garden, but it speaks to me nonetheless. Visitors are able to not just look at the garden, but be in the garden and part of it. Whenever I have taken the time to sit by our little goldfish pond or on a bench in the shady

> *Clematis viorna ×texensis* hybrid.

woodland, or even in the hammock, taking in the gorgeous scenery of color and shape, I become aware of the tremendous amount of life going on around me. With every year, the whole spectrum of insect and bird life has increased enormously. Our plant addiction has paid off in diversity, not just of the plants but animal life as well. With the ever-increasing variety of plant life, food sources for animals and places to hide and nest have correspondingly increased.

Being seated and at rest, I am so much more attuned to a world we so often pass by without noticing, and it is such a busy world. Myriad wasps, bees, flies, bugs, and spiders, all with a mission to collect food for themselves and their brood, from the tiniest metallic green solitary wasp to the striped big bomber bumblebee. There are assassins in the form of a white spider lurking among petals, or a super aggressive wasp trying to take a bee home for dinner. Our patio, with its open view into the rockery and a background of coniferous and deciduous trees, serves as a grand theater. We watch aerial battles. Jet fighters of diminutive stature clash in daring dives and attacks, especially in the season of orange kniphofia and red crocosmia bloom. There is plenty of nectar for each hummingbird, but it is so much more fun to show off, and it is great entertainment for us. We can listen to the distinctive songs of tanagers and robins, we can watch cedar waxwings and phoebes dance and swoop, catching mayflies over the irrigation pool. With this much entertainment, we rarely go to town.

. . .

The grand, open view from the patio to the south now encompasses the mounds of our rock garden building venture of the past, surrounded by a backdrop of shrubs and trees, ending with a distant view of the forest beyond.

A large red oak shades part of the patio in the morning; a Japanese maple gives shade in the afternoon. The dry root zone of the oak is an ideal habitat for *Daphne odora* and *Daphne ×burkwoodii* 'Moonlight Sonata'. These considerations of shade and sun are important aspects of building the garden, since we like to have an open view to take in skies and clouds, trees and flowers. It is hard to believe now that this was a cow pasture and pear orchard. Carpeting plants and conifers in bonsai shapes, mostly forms of Hinoki cypress (*Chamaecyparis obtusa*), cover the central rockery—nothing is too tall to arrest the view.

To the west, the rock garden meets the bamboo hedge and woodland garden. The western part of the alpine beds now lies in deep shade. Beware of labels such as these: "Grows to 6 feet in 10 years." *Ulmus ×hollandica* 'Jacqueline Hillier' was labeled as a rock garden miniature. At first I mistook its enthusiastic growth as a reversion and pruned it back hard like a parent trying to chastise an unruly child. The tree won, just as children often do. I faithfully thin and shape its now 15-by-20-foot winter skeleton. We have come to a peaceful agreement. It cannot grow taller than my ladder and climbing ability will allow, and I will let it be a tree, spreading its branches wider than high. What a beauty it is.

< *Hydrangea anomala* subsp. *petiolaris* var. *cordifolia* 'Brookside Littleleaf' trunks encircling the empty space of a long-gone laburnum tree.

Daphne ×burkwoodii 'Moonlight Sonata'.

Fuchsia 'David' at the foot of the oak.

The alpines underneath the elm have given way to a carpet of shade-lovers and early spring bulbs. Our best forms of purple-red flowered *Trillium kurabayashii* are happy here, surrounded by epimediums, glossy *Polystichum neolobatum*, and creeping *Blechnum wattsii*, an intriguing fern with red emerging fronds. *Saxifraga* 'Dentata' (×*polita*) and *S. stolonifera* 'Rubra', with dainty white flower panicles, creep along, producing new offshoots in a green carpet of mossy *Selaginella kraussiana*. We have found that the large-flowered, bright blue 'Sentimental Blue' platycodon, short in stature and flowering in midsummer, blooms here much longer with larger flowers than it does in the sun.

Small pink and white fuchsias are ideal companions, blooming all summer long, and are far less thirsty here than they are in containers. I am enchanted by all the new varieties of fuchsia available in every garden center and, even when labeled as annuals, appear to be much hardier than they are said to be. Every year they grow bushier. I need to be patient in spring since they are late risers. I never lift them in winter, only shoveling a little molehill of compost over their crown. I cut the old branches after they have frozen to the ground, not before. Maybe someday we will have a winter without frost.

Where this now named 'Jacqueline Hillier' bed slopes slightly to the path, summer watering has created a wet seep. *Epipactis gigantea* 'Serpentine Night' moved at a slow pace into this seep from the center of the bed. This western native orchid, black-leaved and colonizing, found its perfect spot. Planted first in drier parts where it languished, it drifted downward, the rhizomes sensing water, and flourished.

< Shade-giving oak tree (*Quercus rubra*) with a golden ghost bramble beneath (*Rubus cockburnianus* 'Aureus').

Rock garden view to the
south with large conifers in
the background.

Saxifraga stolonifera 'Rubra' in bloom under *Ulmus ×hollandica* 'Jacqueline Hillier'.

How could we have a bed, any bed in the garden, excepting tall perennial borders, without hellebores? And so here. Black- and apricot-flowered varieties make an impressive duo at the south side, ending in a big patch of brilliant, sunny yellow heather where the elm branches don't reach and the sun holds sway all day.

· · ·

Rockeries in English gardens became the grand fashion when collecting alpines became the obsession of Victorian explorers and plant collectors of the British Empire. Soon after, the most difficult treasures were being grown

< The shady side of the rockery looking toward the bamboo to the west.

Corydalis flexuosa and *Polystichum neolobatum* under the elm (*Ulmus ×hollandica* 'Jacqueline Hillier').

Troughs with dianthus and sempervivums.

in hand-hewn stone troughs, previously used to water farm animals. Beautiful as well as extremely heavy, these containers eventually became extremely rare and expensive, so the modern gardener had need for a substitute. While trying to preserve the look of hand-hewn stone containers, a material called hypertufa solved the problem. Imitating the porous, limestone rock called tufa, often used by alpine gardeners, hypertufa is made from lighter, easily available ingredients, such as peat, perlite, and cement.

Troughs are ideal containers to showcase a collection of very special small plants. The soil mix can be easily adjusted to suit the particular needs of various plants and they have some height and are often raised above ground level, which affords a better view of the tiny treasures. Due to their peat and perlite ingredients, the containers are light and porous. Plants growing over their edge can cling with tiny roots to the outside walls, creating a miniature garden spilling over and down. The soil in our troughs is topped with gravel, either chicken grit #2 from our local feed store or ¼-inch washed gravel, or even pea gravel. This mulch helps to keep plant crowns dry and soil moisture even. Well-placed rocks will add to the appeal of a miniature landscape.

How to Build a Trough

This recipe has served us well for all manner of troughs:

Wearing heavy-duty rubber gloves, mix ⅓ peat, ⅓ perlite, ⅓ Portland cement with a hoe in a wheelbarrow. Add 1 handful of Fibermesh (available in large building supply stores) per bag of cement, which gives greater durability. Slowly pour water into the mix and work it in with the hoe until a ball of rather dryish mix formed with your hand holds together.

Now the fun part: A small trough can be built freestyle without a form. Do not forget to add drainage holes. We use pieces of PVC pipe to create drainage holes, leaving some pipe end exposed to make later removal easier. A bigger trough can be built handful by handful inside or outside a form turned upside-down, such as a large styrofoam box, a heavy cardboard box (with a wire around the outside to prevent a bulge), or a wooden box, or even in a carefully dug hole in the ground (but, remember, you have to get it out!). Let your creative juices flow. Remember to use a piece of plastic, such as a garbage bag, as a liner between your form and the mixed material; otherwise they will become inseparable.

Usually, we let our troughs dry for two or three days before taking off the forms. Remove the PVC pipe marking the drainage holes. Leaving the trough in place, use a screwdriver and metal brush to score and roughly brush the sides and top of the trough until it takes on the look of old stone. Burn off any protruding Fibermesh with a torch, or you can let it deteriorate by itself with time.

Within two weeks, the trough can be moved to its final spot in the garden and elevated, if desired, before filling and planting. It is important to set it a bit above ground level on stones for good drainage. Let your masterpiece cure another week, or more, then wash it well to leach out all salts before planting. Now to choose the plants! Endless choices and combinations await.

Thalictrum tuberosum and sempervivums in a trough.

Anemonella thalictroides f. *rosea* 'Oscar Schoaf'.

Fall crocus (*Sternbergia lutea*) growing at the base of a trough.

For the Love of Hellebores

As years passed and our garden grew larger and lovelier with each season, leaving it each morning to landscape the gardens of others in town was more and more difficult. Our hour of departure got later and later. Just a little weeding and pruning before leaving stretched out into hours, until we were arriving in town shortly before noon and were still cleaning up the gardens of our clients as they were sitting down to dinner. Finally, we arrived at a solution: Why not start a nursery? We could raise the plants we loved and needed for landscaping jobs and stay home longer. With the urging and advice of our nursery-owner friend Roger Gossler, we ventured into the retail nursery business. We specialized in more unusual and hard-to-find perennials and shrubs. The retail business expanded for seventeen years until hellebores filled our greenhouses and there was no more room, water, or time to raise other plants for sale. Hellebores took over our life, too. Our business became a hellebore breeding facility and wholesale nursery.

During my early gardening years, I had not been very impressed by the hellebores that were then called *Helleborus orientalis* and are now called *H. ×hybridus*. Of sturdy constitution but with undistinguished greenish, muddy-colored flowers, they were usually relegated to the back of woodland gardens and bloomed at the end of winter when no one noticed. How things have changed. Since about 1945, gardeners, especially in England, have been at work developing better color strains by hybridizing about a dozen species

< *Helleborus* 'Anna's Red'.

Helleborus ×*sternii*, cream and pink types, showing their *H. argutifolius* and *H. lividus* heritage.

Closeup of the features of *Helleborus* ×*sternii*.

of acaulescent species hellebores. We received our first seeds of some of these promising new cultivars from Will McLewin in England and Gisela Schmiemann in Germany in the early 1990s. Soon afterward, *The Gardener's Guide to Growing Hellebores* (1993) was published with photos of brightly colored flowers in various hues. We were smitten and intrigued. We were drawn to Europe on a pilgrimage to the best hellebore nurseries, which initiated our addiction to hellebores now in its twenty-fifth year.

Hellebore, also known as Lenten rose, belongs to the buttercup family (Ranunculaceae) and is divided into two main groups that are, for the most part, genetically incompatible with each other. Members of *Helleborus* ×*hybridus* and their species ancestors belong to the acaulescent, or stemless, group. They have no true stem (leaf and flower stalks don't count) and hybridize freely with each other. The other group, called caulescent, or stemmed, consists of *H. argutifolius*, the tallest, from Corsica, *H. lividus* from Spain, *H. niger*, or the Christmas rose, having underground stems, and *H. foetidus*, the loner, which doesn't cross with any other species but is widespread in Europe. We grow a form of *H. foetidus* with intensely pewter-colored leaves, which loves drought and full sun and is not long-lived but reseeds itself. The most common of the stemmed

group, *H.* ×*sternii*, is actually a hybrid of *H. argutifolius* and *H. lividus*. Look closely and you will see that flowers and leaves emerge from a true stem.

In February, 2004, we set out for Europe and our first trip to Ashwood Nurseries, in Kingswinford, England, the Mecca of all hellebore lovers. We traveled with Dick and Judith Tyler, owners of Pine Knot Farms in Virginia, and fellow hellebore addict, Cole Burrell. Judith and Cole subsequently published the invaluable *Hellebores: A Comprehensive Guide* (2006). We searched in England, Holland, and Germany for the finest *Helleborus* ×*hybridus* then being bred. At Ashwood, we were permitted to select from all their pre-sale plants, but with a caveat. Kevin Belcher, their outstanding hellebore breeder, would examine our choice selections with his discerning eye and take back whatever plant he saw as a fitting candidate for his own breeding program. Watching him take back an elegant, black-flowered specimen or a choice yellow was an agonizing moment. We did, though, return with many excellent plants of then-rare colors from Ashwood and other outstanding European nurseries. We shipped a trove of flowering hellebores home. They survived the bare-rooting, the inspections, and more than a week in transit, all while in bloom.

We dreamed of breeding ever better and brighter hellebore flowers with good foliage to match. We

Helleborus ×hybridus with the deep yellow color of Winter Jewels Golden Sunrise.

Helleborus ×hybridus Winter Jewels Blue Diamond.

Helleborus ×hybridus Winter Jewels Amethyst Gem, a dark purple-red with a narrow pink edge on its sepals.

Helleborus ×hybridus Winter Jewels Picotee Pearl, a semi-double flower with a central ruff of red nectaries.

Helleborus ×hybridus Winter Jewels Rose Quartz, a double bloom that shows off the colorful tips of inner petals that look like the tutus of ballerinas.

followed the dreams of our imagination. We bred for a brilliant yellow flower that is slow to turn green, slate flowers that one could call blue with only a bit of a stretch, and shapely flowers with rounded, even sepals and colorful backs that would entice even the casual viewer. Sometimes different colors on the outside and inside can surprise us when lifting a flower head, as in the Winter Jewels examples of purple Amethyst Gem and dark Harlequin Gem. A short petiole raises them to a more vertical position. We love the semi-doubles with nectaries of different shades, truly black flowers, and big, blowsy doubles that hang their heads only to show off the colorful tips of inner petals like the tutus of ballerinas.

We are often asked why we don't strive for up-facing flowers. Like many other early bloomers from winter snowy or rainy climates (think daffodils or snowdrops), these plants must keep their pollen dry so it does not rot and, with it, the flower. Some other smaller flowered early bloomers bend their heads or close their flower when skies turn gray, such as crocus and *Anemone nemorosa*.

We netted our stock houses with shade cloth for our ever-increasing collections and to exclude those pesky bees that would muddy our progeny with their indiscriminate pollinating. They could have a go at the expanding outdoor hellebore plantings. All stock plants are numbered and categorized by color and placed on tables to save our backs.

When seeds start to ripen, each flower is bagged in a small cotton mesh bag so the seeds don't fall on the ground, and we sow the seed thereafter. The next winter we are excited to see the seedlings emerge. One or

> A colorful mix of hellebores.

Helleborus ×hybridus Winter Jewels Cotton Candy, a soft, blush-pink strain.

two years later, following potting and repotting, the first resulting flowers of our breeding work open in February. For us, it is the beginning of a new spring.

In February and March we are open for retail on two weekends of hellebore frenzy. We sell only flowering hellebore plants at that time. We love to see the happy faces of customers who found just what they were looking for: a finely tuned collection to take home, making a little garden on the cart; a bright yellow flower to light up foggy winter days; or a huge 10-year-old pot of a mass of double pinks for the patio.

Hellebores fill many parts of our garden. Late winter and early spring is the time of seemingly endless show-ers and skies in many shades of gray. Just when the endless gray darkens our moods, the hellebores begin to flower. They thrive in cool weather. They bloom in vibrant colors for a good two months. During frost, the flowering stems wilt, releasing water from their cells, only to rise again with warming temperatures. They are truly unstoppable.

What we see as colorful petals are really sepals, like the green bud covers on a rose. The true petals have shrunk to nectaries—small pouch-like appendages filled with nectar. The colorful sepals attract early bees and bumblebees. When temperatures are above 55°F,

the drifts of hellebores are abuzz with insects. The rise in temperature also speeds seed production and the greening of the sepals, which now take on the job of photosynthesis. Our cool springs prolong the bloom of our hellebores.

No other hellebore can compete with the extra-ordinary color range and complexity of flower color of our favorite, *Helleborus ×hybridus*, and of our Winter Jewels hybrids. There are many ways to use the various hellebores in our gardens. Combinations include a bed of no-holds-barred color mix of hellebore flowers, underplanted with *Anemone nemorosa* and snowdrops. In summer, the foliage of the Lenten roses serves as a dense ground cover under vine maple, dogwood, and a large *Corylopsis spicata*. We prune the winter hazel to let in light for the hellebores below.

In other spots, we limit ourselves to more restrained color groupings involving one to three shades of bloom. A voluptuous, heavily flowered, blush pink strain with the look of a rose in winter we named Cotton Candy, because its color and fluffy flowers resemble that frothy confection. We planted several of these in mass between low, silver lamium (*Lamium maculatum* 'Beacon Silver' or 'White Nancy') with a backdrop of *Camellia ×williamsii* 'Donation' blooming at the same

Helleborus ×hybridus Winter Jewels Sparkling Diamond is pure white.

Helleborus ×ericsmithii 'Winter Moonbeam' has exceptional foliage lasting throughout the season.

A robust result of our crossing *Helleborus multifidus* subsp. *hercegovinus* with *H.* ×*hybridus*, shown in full bloom. The finely cut foliage will emerge later.

time in the exact same shade of light pink (think color echo). The pairing gives us great visual satisfaction, not unlike a gourmet being served a five-star meal.

A solid group of pure double whites among low evergreen ferns carries a festive air. Our hellebore strain of bright yellow singles with winter golden foliage (Golden Sunrise and Apricot Blush) look particularly stunning in a bed of black mondo grass (*Ophiopogon planiscapus* 'Nigrescens') or massed under a bigleaf maple out of my kitchen window with a look of sunshine underfoot. Black hellebores (Black Diamond and Blue Diamond) show off especially well with white snowdrops and white *Helleborus* ×*ballardiae* 'Pink Frost', which turns copper-pink with age. *Helleborus* ×*hybridus* Winter Jewels Ruby Wine, with an exceptional deep red color, is best planted backlit by the winter sun, which gives it a glow like a glass of the best red wine held up to the light.

Diseases such as gray mold (*Botrytis cinerea*) and black spot (*Microsphaeropsis hellebori*) can affect hellebores in springs with cold, damp air. Some flowering stems turn black and fuzzy at the crown and keel over.

Individual flowers may shrivel and die. Hygiene is most important. On our daily garden walks, we carry clippers and a bucket to cut and dispose of any diseased tissue. Botrytis kills what it touches, so we remove all affected stems and flowers. We clean our clippers with rubbing alcohol (isopropanol), which kills fungus spores.

Black spot fungus does not kill, except in severe cases, but it sprinkles flowers and leaves with unsightly black spots, especially visible on pure white specimens, and mars their looks.

Some organic approved fungicide preventatives are available, such as Oxidate 2 (strong hydrogen peroxide) or Cease (a bacterial product). We have noticed that some individual plants have more genetic affinity to fungus diseases year after year. We give them three years, and if the problem recurs each spring, we dig them out and deposit them in the garbage. If it is a stock plant, it meets the same fate.

The only serious insect problem we have noticed on hellebores is aphids. Aphids are such a ubiquitous garden pest that most people have their favorite

Some of the *Helleborus multifidus* ×*hybridus* hybrids carry finely cut leaves with a silvery sheen in spring.

methods of control, either systemic or nonsystemic contact control.

Hellebores thrive on deciduous woodland slopes or in shaded clearings among shrubs or rocks. They prefer a position in semi-shade (dense shade can reduce flowering) with rich, moist, but not waterlogged soil. Fertilize with organic fertilizer when planting. If possible, plant hellebores on a sloping bed, both to improve drainage and to make it easier to look into the nodding flowers. A well-established hellebore plant can become a clump about 18 to 22 inches tall and wide.

Although tolerant of soil type, hellebores are deep-rooted, and to flower at their best, they appreciate plenty of nutrients and adequate moisture. We mix a handful of organic fertilizer, such as Bio Fish, into their planting hole. We mulch with compost containing well-rotted animal manure in late fall or winter. Don't bury the crown! You can also use slow-release fertilizer around the plant.

Remove the old, faded flower stems in early May, unless you require seed, to encourage next years

developing new growth. Remove all foliage from hybrid hellebores and the deciduous species in December or January to improve the appearance of the plant (the old leaves eventually die, slowly), to make it easier to see the flowers, and to prevent the spread of any existing fungal disease to the newly emerging flowers, stems, and leaves.

Hellebores do not need to be divided, but if you wish to transplant or divide a clump, the task is best done in September or October. Dividing is best accomplished by digging up the whole plant, washing the crown free of soil so you can see what you are doing, and then cutting between the growth buds with a sharp knife. Leave at least three buds in each division and replant in well-draining mix or soil.

In recent years, new, sterile hybrids of *Helleborus sternii*, *lividus*, and *niger* have emerged from tissue culture, with many more to come. Several show lovely, marbled foliage, such as *H.* ×*ericsmithii* (it may actually be ×*ballardiae*) 'Winter Moonbeam'. The vigorous green-leaved selection *H.* ×*ballardiae* 'Pink Frost' bears cream-white flowers turning copper-pink with age.

Helleborus ×hybridus Winter Jewels Onyx Odyssey.

The true species *Helleborus orientalis*, from wild-collected seed in Turkey. Spring foliage is a deep red-bronze.

Helleborus ×hybridus Winter Jewels Apricot Blush.

Helleborus ×*hybridus* Winter Jewels Fire and Ice, a recent result in our breeding program.

A new introduction from Rodney Davey in England is named 'Anna's Red' for its prominent red flowers. It is a large plant with silver-streaked leaves, combining for the first time stemmed (caulescent) and stemless (acaulescent) hellebores in a hybrid. It took twelve years of breeding efforts to come up with this complex, beautiful hybrid. We planted several groupings in woodland and shady rockery. The remarkable silver variegation of the leaves does not fade with age.

After many years, our crossing *Helleborus multifidus* subsp. *hercegovinus* with *H.* ×*hybridus*, has resulted in robust, bushy plants with narrow, many-segmented leaflets. They grace the garden in partly shaded areas in fertile soil. These hybrids are evergreen and carry flowers in purple, green, and chartreuse-yellow. With age, their leaflets become more and more divided until they almost look like a large green feather duster. We love to grow them among plants with coarser foliage, such as pulmonarias and epimediums, with the giant *Tetrapanax papyrifer* 'Steroidal Giant' spreading its umbrella-like leaves above.

Our one plant of the true *Helleborus orientalis* from the Aladağ Mountains of Turkey, grown from wild-collected seed, surprised us with its deep red-bronze foliage in spring. Single white flowers grace the plant in late winter. The foliage turns green with the onset of warm weather, and it is spectacular in spring. *Helleborus orientalis* is also native to other places, such as northeast Greece and Caucasian Russia. This plant is a very unusual form for the species, with its red leaves.

Our selection of *Helleborus foetidus* 'Red Silver', with its pewter-colored leaves and red petioles, can be grown for the beauty of foliage alone. It does best in full sun and poor, dry soil, which makes it an ideal plant for the strip along sidewalks.

Many gardeners consider hellebores to be the perfect plant, for several reasons: They bloom on dreary winter days. They are deer-proof. They are evergreen. They grow in clay, silt, or sandy soil. They grow in either shade or sun (in the Pacific Northwest). They can handle drought. And they are very beautiful. What more could we want?

the
perennial
borders

THE PERENNIAL BORDERS are not directly visible from the windows of the house, but come as a surprise when taking the path from the back door. An almost straight path of flat, irregular stepping stones runs through the center of two of the perennial borders, and that path is crossed by two other paths at right angles. The view lines are laid out in a formal pattern bisected by round stone mosaics at the axis of the paths. When standing at the end of the paths we enjoy a long view line of flowering perennials from late spring through fall.

But what about winter when perennials are dormant and the beds mostly empty? We then realized that some woody plants could enhance the borders year-round and also lessen the high maintenance somewhat when old age creeps up on us. Someday we might want to ease off a bit on the intense care required for a sunny perennial border. So we planted some small decorative trees, or at least they were small at planting time, and now have grown larger than their labels had us believe at purchase time. The elegant *Cornus controversa* 'Variegata' with its tiered branches, aptly called wedding cake tree, now shades a once sunny bed. Over the years we have adjusted the perennial plantings accordingly.

< Side entry to the perennial borders.

Coleus and podophyllum on shady north side of the side entrance to the perennial borders.

Cypripedium kentuckiense.

These borders are meant to be colorful from spring until frost, which often in the Pacific Northwest does not arrive until November, or even December. The beds on the north side of the path glow in summer with vivid oranges, yellows, and reds of crocosmias, dark-leaved red and yellow dahlias, heliopsis and goldenrod, with yellow and orange lilies sprinkled in between. *Geranium psilostemon* and blue *Geranium* 'Rozanne' as well as a dark-purple phlox offer contrast, and a few white lilies as well as the white, fragrant *Hydrangea angustipetala* 'MonLong Shou' and white *Clematis recta* give a bit of visual relief.

One end of the border is edged with weeping yellow Japanese forest grass (*Hakonechloa macra* 'All Gold'), and the other end is occupied with black mondo grass. Our favorite green and yellow variegated *Cornus sericea* 'Hedgerows Gold' and sumac (*Rhus typhina* 'Tiger Eyes') add even more golden yellow in a shrubby way. A big hardy banana (*Musa basjoo*) dominates it all with its enormous fan-like leaves on stems to 15 feet. Two clipped, variegated *Salix integra* 'Hakuro-nishiki' on standards add pizzazz. There is plenty of lush, soothing green in the form of two trees grown for fall color, *Parrotia persica* 'Vanessa' and an umbrella-shaped black tupelo, *Nyssa sylvatica* 'Autumn Cascades', to balance out all the wild colors. I find the hot colors very stimulating and so do the hummingbirds that fly between the red and orange flowers like little jet fighters.

Some of our favorite small trees for borders are *Acer circinatum* 'Pacific Fire'; *A. japonica* 'Aconitifolium'; *A. palmatum* 'Mikawa-yatsubusa'; *A. palmatum*

« previous pages: View of the entrance to the perennial borders in spring.

> *Euphorbia cyparissias,* best kept in a container because it can become very invasive.

Center of the perennial garden with a pebble mosaic by Portland artist Jeffrey Bale.

'Shishigashira'; *Cornus mas* and *C. mas* 'Variegata'; *Stewartia pseudocamellia* var. *koreana*; *S. malacodendron*; *Styrax obassia*; and *S. japonicus* 'Evening Light'.

Look to the south of the path and all is restful under the shade of the *Cornus controversa* 'Variegata', echoing, with its tiered variegated foliage, the two willows (*Salix integra* 'Hakuro-nishiki') across from it. In the shade of the dogwood and a 'Sekkan-sugi' cryptomeria, live shade perennials with flowers of softer tones and hues among ferns and podophyllums. The tango next door has been toned down to a minuet. Astrantias mingle with pink *Thalictrum rochebrunnianum*, *Pimpinella major* 'Rosea', and white *Gillenia trifoliata*. Blue phlox and delphiniums grow in the sunnier parts of the border with soft pink dahlias and blue *Clematis* 'Rhapsody'. In spring as well as in fall, the leaves

Cornus sericea 'Hedgerows Gold'.

of two of the red-stemmed *Hydrangea macrophylla* 'Lady in Red' will take on a copper-red hue while the flowers bloom a soft pink in our soil.

The five perennial beds encompass about 2,200 square feet and are roughly rectangular. I say roughly because even though they are basically a formal design, my nature cannot easily accommodate exactness. I meander on a line between order and disorder and feel quite comfortable on it. Harmonious disorder is my comfort zone. So, the paths and bed edges also meander a bit and are only almost straight with slight sinuous bends.

The beds color in spring with innumerable dark blue chionodoxa, sky blue *Scilla hispanica,* and many varieties of *Anemone nemorosa*. Sadly, I long ago had to abandon the idea of tulips and crocus. Hundreds or thousands of voles from

Allium carinatum subsp. *pulchellum* with purple and white forms among sedums.

Asiatic lily 'Giraffe' in the perennial bed.

Pimpinella major 'Rosea' with *Corydalis flexuosa* hybrids under *Cornus controversa* 'Variegata'.

Clematis recta and C. 'Rooguchi'.

< *Cornus controversa* 'Variegata' with *Hydrangea macrophylla* 'Lady in Red'.

Clematis 'Multi Blue' in *Wisteria frutescens* var. *macrostachya* 'Blue Moon'.

the surrounding meadows have found a better meal than grass seeds in our garden. Many bulbs do not even last through one flowering. We had to learn what voles find appetizing and what they eschew. Sometimes their favorite is a certain strain within the same species, usually the rarer or more expensive one, it seems. These little fat rodents are quite discerning. So, we grow what we can and have learned not to lose our temper (except now and then). In May the glorious round balls of flowering onions appear. Pinks, blues, violets, and whites of all heights and sizes create a joyous spring dance before the heavyweights of summer appear.

We were enticed by a photo of a glowing, acid yellow, bracted umbellifer *Smyrnium perfoliatum* in *Christopher Lloyd's Flower Garden* book. We set about obtaining seed. *Smyrnium perfoliatum* is a monocarpic tuber. It takes three or more years to bloom from seed. It sets plentiful black seed and then dies. The trick is to sow some seed each year initially to stagger flowering, but then watch out! It self-sows with abandon, and like *Anthriscus sylvestris* 'Ravenswing', needs careful removal after flowering before seeds are completely ripe and drop. In the first year, a pair of cotyledons appears, producing a tiny white tuber. In the following year or two, it looks more like a celery leaf, dying down by

midsummer. Then comes the glorious flowering year. It is treasured by flower arrangers and gardeners alike.

Smyrnium perfoliatum.

Over the many years the alliums have multiplied in the rich compost to such an extent that they are now neck to neck. Voles apparently do not care for onions. We cut or pull out the foliage as soon as it starts browning and leave only the flowering stalk standing. This also gives the summer blooming perennials just emerging breathing room to push through the field of alliums. At this point we set up gridded, grow-through supports of various dimensions for those flowering plants we know would topple later on. (Some plants that can benefit from support are: baptisia, *Actaea matsumurae* 'White Pearl' (syn. *Cimicifuga* 'The Pearl'), dahlia, delphinium, *Geranium* 'Rozanne', gillenia, large geraniums, phlox, tall asters, and veronicastrum.) As soon as the plant tips grow through the supports, the green painted supports are no longer visible and the plant looks as if it stands gracefully on its own.

high summer in the perennial borders

LAZY, BLOWSY SUMMER days are here. It is midsummer and the five perennial borders are in full exuberant growth. Six-foot-tall, bright yellow Asiatic lilies have been blooming all through midsummer together with brilliant *Crocosmia* 'Lucifer', and yet the lilies show no signs of fading until early August when they shed their last flowers. *Crocosmia ×crocosmiiflora* 'Star of the East', interplanted among them, carries on the show through late summer. Dark blue *Veronica longifolia* 'Marietta', bought solely for sentimental reasons because my sister's name is Veronika, makes a beautiful counterpoint to the red crocosmia and yellow heliopsis daisies. The turf and black mondo grass–lined path has become narrower, as it does every year around this time. Since our garden isn't a public garden, I like the Japanese idea of minor obstructions in the path to slow the hurried gardener or visitor and encourage a closer look at blooms and fluttering swallowtails or velvet-coated bumblebees sipping nectar.

Bold or strident, depending upon one's sensibilities, is the theme in this particular border. Hidden behind the stout banana, a patch of magenta-flowered phlox appears, intermingled with the same 'Lucifer' and backed by the vigorous golden sumac, 'Tiger Eyes', with lots of luscious green between. After the initial shock wears off, I find

< View of central perennial path in high summer.

Helmeted *Eucomis bicolor* guarding the entrance.

Central path looking west, with *Salix integra* 'Hakuro-nishiki'.

it invigorating, as long as it does not repeat to the point of visual exhaustion. Just like a rich dessert, a little is tasty, too much is cloying.

Across the central path lies the south flower bed shaded by two dogwoods and a stewartia. The entrance is marked by a large grouping of pineapple-helmeted racemes of starry-flowered *Eucomis bicolor*, dressed in skirts of strap-shaped leaves, looking bold and purposeful. Here, as in all woodland gardens, life has taken on green, quieter summer tones—a restful contrast. Late-blooming, tall and dainty, *Thalictrum delavayi*, with lacy leaves, has umbels of foamy pink on 6- to 8-foot stems that reach up through tree branches and drape themselves over black-leaved pink dahlias. The best and

Yellow Asiatic lilies and *Veronica longifolia* 'Marietta'.

latest of the foam flowers is the double-flowered, albeit sterile, form, 'Hewitt's Double', hard to find but well worth searching for at specialty nurseries.

Blue-flowered *Clematis* 'Rhapsody' layers itself over and through two onion-domed obelisks at each end of the bed. With a maximum height of 6 feet, 'Rhapsody', blooming all summer, never outgrows its support, but with its dense habit covers it with a flower-studded mantle from top to bottom. Heavenly scented oriental trumpet lily 'Silk Road' is planted throughout the bed. Six feet tall, with enormous white flowers and crimson-pink throats, its beauty and fragrance have made it one of the most popular lilies in northwest gardens. Its flowers last longer in semi-shade. In the darkest areas under

Stewartia sinensis.

Lilium 'Silk Road' (Orienpet lily).

the trees grow summer-flowering *Kirengeshoma palmata*, maidenhair ferns, painted fern, and silver-centered *Arisaema consanguineum*, offering a change from the masses of blue delphiniums of earlier sun-drenched years when the trees were newly planted.

How different the perennial beds appear now than in late spring. The vigor of erect spring growth has given way to full-flowered buxomness of leaning, mingling, sprawling growth. The invisible hand of the gardener has created magic. What looks like a spontaneous creation of flowers sharing space, of colors that complement each other is an illusion that is a large part of the art of gardening. Dill seed from the adjacent vegetable garden sowed itself into the flowerbeds and became a masterful ingredient, tall, narrow umbels creating a bond between coarser leaved perennials. *Allium christophii*, vivid, metallic magenta in spring, now with straw-colored umbels, is left standing, holding up taller neighbors at the front of the border, until it finally disperses its seed and topples.

Three more perennial beds along this path show no sign of the summer doldrums. Growth is so dense that most weeds are relegated to the lower darkness and a very thin existence. Deadheading and preventing seed production in order to prolong the flowering season are now the gardener's most pressing chores. Sometimes a weaker plant needs to be rescued from an over-vigorous embrace of a burly neighbor.

A long, 25-foot clematis and honeysuckle–covered trellis separates the third perennial bed from the kitchen garden hidden behind it. Single-flowered

> *Dahlia* 'Forncett Furnace', bright orange and tall, with *Dahlia* 'Mystic Illusion' and *Hibiscus syriacus* 'White Chiffon' in foreground.

^ *Phygelius* 'Passionate'.
⌃ *Lilium* 'Rio Negro' (Oriental lily).

^ Dahlia, grown from a self-sown seedling.
⌃ Golden sumac (*Rhus typhina* 'Tiger Eyes'), fennel plant, with a backdrop of a hardy banana (*Musa basjoo*).

dahlias, asters, salvias, verbascums, and coneflowers are the mainstay of this bed. *Dahlia* 'Forncett Furnace', a brassy 7-foot orange eyeful impossible to overlook, forms the backdrop to black *Actaea simplex* 'James Compton', dark red Cape fuchsia, and an edging of black mondo grass. Reblooming 'Lyda Rose' clothes the opposite end of this bed in white and blush pink. Black foliage of the 'James Compton' is repeated with *Symphyotrichum lateriflorum* 'Prince'. Masses of tiny blooms adorn the aster come fall. Earlier on, Asiatic lilies, alliums, and dark-colored opium poppies dominated. A big, pink-flowered, now purple-fruited crabapple 'Beanpole' has fleshed out over the years and no longer lives up to its name.

The same can be said about the neighbors across the path. Two purple *Berberis thunbergii* f. *atropurpurea* 'Helmond Pillar' plants flank this bed. They have

Dill seedling and red *Crocosmia* 'Lucifer'.

Crocosmia ×*crocosmiiflora* 'Star of the East' and annual (in our climate) *Lantana camara*.

surrendered their youthful, slim figures to a portly middle age. I cinch their belts by hard winter pruning. This bed is centered by a black weeping tupelo tree, 'Autumn Cascades', and planted on the sunny side with huge, bright yellow and red trumpet lilies, dahlias, and a mass of *Crocosmia* ×*crocosmiiflora* 'Star of the East'. This, the largest flowered of all the crocosmias, orange with a light throat, is a late summer bloomer, its buds opening in August.

Various crocosmias can stretch the bloom season from June through September. Starting in June with red *Crocosmia* 'Lucifer', it continues with the yellows such as 'Citronella', followed by bright orange, mahogany-throated 'Emily McKenzie', light orange 'Star of the East', and ending with the smaller, nonspreading 'Solfatare', with sulfur-tinged green leaves and apricot-yellow flower spikes. All varieties are hummingbird magnets.

A hint: If you are worried about the spreading talents of crocosmias, each winter after frosts, at cleanup time, cut crocosmias to about 1 foot and not to the ground. With the bed bare, it is easy to fork up unwanted bulbs. There is always a demand in the neighborhood, much more than for giant zucchini.

A merry mix of colors surrounds the weeping tupelo. Cream and green, variegated foliage and purple-magenta flowers adorn *Phlox paniculata* 'Harlequin',

Wasps feeding on the nectar of *Eryngium planum*.
This variety of wasp feeds only on eryngium.

Purple and white alliums, blue larkspur, and red
nasturtiums.

best with a little afternoon shade and plenty of water. Blue *Eryngium alpinum*, humming with bees, and a big, dark-flowered eucomis make a great mix. In this garden, it is hard to talk about midsummer blooming as studied combinations. Intuition is a gardener's best companion. Some satisfying combinations in the not-so-dog-days of summer are the black-leaved, crimson-red dahlia 'Mystic Enchantment' and an equally velvet red nasturtium, a bit of straw-colored *Allium christophii*, and yellow *Hypericum 'Kolmoran'* Mystical Orange. A little self-sown larkspur here and there and the white, scented, *Nicotiana sylvestris* for evening pleasure, for both moth and man, are enriched by black mondo grass at the edges of the bed.

For the aspiring summer-flower gardener, I recommend standing in front of your beds in spring and imagining shapes and colors of summer that will be pleasing to you. Then go to your spring plant sales armed with a vision for your summer garden. It may not all work out at first, but an undaunted gardener will try until utmost satisfaction is achieved. Don't be swayed or intimidated by fads and fashion; the garden is there to please you, the gardener, first of all.

One of the most magnificent plants in our summer border is *Zantedeschia* 'Flame' with giant, silver-shot leaves, and, as its name suggests, flaming spathes in red and yellow. Many years ago I acquired a brilliant, true red Oriental poppy, 'Tango', in Germany. But Oriental poppies bloom in May, and then leave a big hole in the summer border as they go dormant. I spent much time meditating

Red oriental poppy 'Tango' (*Papaver orientale* 'Tango').

Zantedeschia 'Flame' growing in the same spot as *Papaver orientale* 'Tango', but in midsummer.

on that hole. Calla lilies, on the other hand, only rise from giant tubers in June. So, there was the answer. Two plants, one spot. They have been excellent companions ever since.

In the center of these beds lies Jeffrey Bale's pebble mosaic, our magic circle. The mosaic represents the four seasons of the year. Here, we sleep on starry nights surrounded by the most fragrant flowers: Oriental lilies and night-flowering tobacco (*Nicotiana sylvestris*). At daybreak we are awakened by daring, fearless, territorial little hummingbird fighters, each claiming every flower of the thousands that surround us. Our red pillowcases and blue sleeping bag are of special interest and warrant close, darting inspections. Honeybees and bumblebees use the central path as a flyway between tall flowers, and zoom by, very goal-oriented or, at least, seeming to know exactly where they are going.

From where we sleep on the mosaic, we look directly at two tall and narrow Alaskan weeping cedars, *Chamaecyparis nootkatensis* 'Van den Akker', the guardians of the vegetable garden though they have never intimidated vole, mole, or raccoon. We use these narrow, graceful trees in many areas of the garden. Birds love their tips as lookouts over their territory; we love their slender, weeping, evergreen forms swaying in the lightest breeze.

The easternmost perennial bed is backed by a weeping silver pear and flanked by two tall *Viburnum plicatum* f. *tomentosum* 'Pink Beauty'. After a good show of white flowers in spring, aging to pink, the viburnum is decorated

with bright red berries, and a purple-blue *Clematis* 'Blue Belle' covers it with a mantle of flowers until fall. The dense, willow-leaved pear (*Pyrus salicifolia* 'Pendula') is an excellent backdrop to perennial borders. Its silver foliage enhances every other nearby color. Its thick branching habit makes a beautiful silver screen in summer, but come winter its densely unattractive, Medusa-like head of snaking, tangled branches becomes all too visible. Thinning cleans out dead and aging wood and makes for exuberant new silver growth, come summer. Its angular branches, though, do not result in a graceful form, no matter how skilled the pruner may be.

Airy companions front the pear, such as grasses, *Persicaria polymorpha*, re-blooming *Delphinium* 'Völkerfrieden', *Thalictrum delavayi*, and *Geranium* 'Rozanne'. Asiatic lilies spend their beauty in June, while Oriental and trumpet lilies scent the garden in July and August. I like the very tallest and strongly stemmed, like some of the orienpet hybrids, growing 6 to 7 feet, dominating all the other tall-flowering perennials. They are the favorite lookout perches of our hummingbirds.

Entrance to the vegetable garden to the south guarded by two Alaskan cedars (*Chamaecyparis nootkatensis* 'Van den Akker').

This bed continues with more single-flowered red and yellow dahlias having the blackest foliage I can find, such as the Mystic series like 'Flame' or 'Desire'. Shrub rose 'Radway Sunrise' flashes rays of sunrise and sunset in a blend of lemon, salmon, and coral in its single-flowered clusters. This cultivar, introduced in 1962 in England, is very disease resistant. Tea roses and the large double-flowered varieties of highly bred dahlias would not fit in this garden. They are too stiff in form to be neighborly and are best used when showcasing their flowers in an orderly cutting garden. Good weavers and binders hold this bed together: blue 'Rozanne', longest flowering of the geranium tribe, as well as purple-pink pea-flowered *Lespedeza thunbergii* 'Samidare', and the ever-present *Thalictrum delavayi*, a welcome seeder in every bed, and purple-blue phlox.

Perennial border with *Chamaecyparis nootkatensis* 'Van den Akker' in the background.

Hypericum 'Kolmoran' Mystical Orange.

This is our summertime garden, with ample seating in the shade of the old Bosc pear, or under the trellis of a purple grape (*Vitis vinifera* 'Purpurea'), or even from the platform of our newly built treehouse. Our son built it for the grandkids, on top of the large stump of a walnut tree, but grandma and grandpa may relax here too, as long as we can climb the staircase to it. It affords a very different view of the garden than from ground level, in addition to a sleeping platform with a grand view of the stars during summer nights.

To the east, a row of little cone-shaped, pruned boxwoods lines the path behind the silver pear and viburnums, and then a whole different view, hidden by trees, greets us—an entirely separate universe. We go from lush English garden to the dry and sunny Southwest in a journey that takes only five steps. We are still in the Pacific Northwest, but transported to the Southwest in spirit with the entrance to the chaparral garden.

< Entrance to the chaparral garden from the perennial borders.

the
chaparral
garden

INSPIRED BY OUR many hikes in the deserts of California, Oregon, and Utah, as well as the mountains of Tasmania and the high-altitude Drakensburg in South Africa, we dreamed of bringing some of this look home to our valley in western Oregon. We wanted the warm scent of pines, the brilliant burst of color of seasonal flowers resembling a mountain meadow in bloom, yet a bloom prolonged throughout summer. We were drawn to the aesthetics of dryland chaparral: shrubs of small stature with drought-tolerant perennials and bulbs planted beneath. Was this too much to ask? Gardeners today have the advantage of sampling plants from every corner of the world with similar climates, thanks to the many dedicated plant explorers and nurseries.

Our site is blessed with a backdrop of native Douglas fir and oaks and a view of the forested hills beyond. The occasional howl of coyotes, cries of the hawks, chattering of jays, and cawing of crows all connect the garden and our man-made chaparral with the wider landscape. Any see-through fencing we need to use for chickens, peacocks, and deer is built to blend and leave no visual barrier. We wanted the structural look of the montane chaparral combined with the green lushness of western Oregon, a chaparral garden on steroids with the ability to withstand a gray, rainy winter season.

< Chaparral garden in summer with blooming perennials and conifers, with the old chicken house in the background.

Chaparral garden in early summer.

It became a voyage of discovery. We learned that coming through our wet winters would be more of a challenge for these plants than so-called hardiness. What can be grown in colder winters with prolonged sunshine and relative dry conditions may not thrive here. The reputed hardiness zone of a plant does not tell the whole story. The combination of wet and extreme cold, lasting sometimes for many days, often spells death to agaves, callistemons, grevilleas. Plants from mountains of South Africa, Tasmania and New Zealand, and South America are often not reliably hardy because of our prolonged low temperatures combined with wet.

• • •

We first planted low-growing conifer cultivars and a sampling of plants from the Southwest to give us an outline of the garden to be. To avoid a flat, even look as a result of the uniform pebble mulch, and to give the planting a naturalistic feel, we brought home decayed conifer wood and rocks from road construction areas during our mountain excursions and placed them haphazardly in among the plantings. They enrich the garden with the texture of Nature and create moisture pockets.

Small cultivars of the western Ponderosa pine and any of the very slow varieties of bristlecone pine (*Pinus aristata*), decorated with white pitch pockets,

A peacock showing off on the other side of the chaparral garden fence.

Chaparral garden in fall with a view to the west toward the conifer garden. Deciduous *Taxodium distichum* has already taken on rust-colored fall tones.

are favorites. One cultivar was curiously named 'Great Guy'. We found a place here too for our mountain hemlock, *Tsuga mertensiana*. It thrives with some summer drought and full sun. Small trees for chaparral gardens include: *Chamaecyparis* spp., *Diospyros* spp., *Quercus* spp., *Pinus aristata* and cultivars, *Pinus parviflora* cultivars, and *Pinus ponderosa* dwarf cultivars.

California species of manzanitas, with smooth mahogany bark and covered in terminal clusters of pink or white flowers in spring, used to be considered impossible to grow since any transplant from the wild promptly died and pot-grown plants were unavailable. Wonderful cutting-grown varieties from California and Oregon nurseries have changed all that. Now many species and selections are available—mounding and compact, sparse and tall, blue foliage or dark green—the choice is ours. My favorite manzanita is 'Howard McMinn', a dense, mound-forming shrub and a prolific bloomer with masses of pink-tinged white flowers in spring. Manzanitas are evergreen. Drainage must be perfect and water scarce for these residents.

Then there are the bottlebrushes (*Callistemon*) from Australia, with red, yellow, or green spikes of tiny flowers, looking, yes, like a bottlebrush. We have had mild winters with a sudden dip to 0°F, what we call an Alaskan express, with winds from the north, when all the bottlebrush shrubs died aboveground, only to resurrect in spring with new growth from below. They are unkillable.

What, at first, was a large empty-looking gravel lot with a small shrub or tree dotted here and there has become so filled with life that each new purchase must be carefully considered. Building a complex, all-year-flowering, lively desert has been a slow process. We started many ground covers and bulbs from seed, and even in the silty, graveled soil the meadow voles invaded, following the ever-present mole tunnels. Choice fritillaries, *Anemone blanda*, tulips, crocuses, and species gladiolus all ended up as morsels for large appe-

Iris reticulata 'George'.

tites. But for year-round beauty, especially in winter and spring, bulbs are essential. So we persisted. We planted so many of *Anemone blanda*, the Greek windflower, which then did us the favor of seeding prolifically, even overwhelming vole predation. They just couldn't find them all!

Dwarf *Iris reticulata*, with blue or purple flowers with yellow highlights, flower so early in the season they would charm anyone. They bloom prolifically at the end of winter in sandy, gravelly soil, and are best grown in dry conditions in summer when they go dormant. But here comes the winter rain! Being from dry mountain regions of the Middle East, their flowers literally melt into a soggy, inky goo in a wet spring. If the rain holds off, we can admire them for a while. As with the peony flower, we absorb its ephemeral beauty and say, 'Thank you'.

We planted cyclamen for longer lasting winter flowers, especially *Cyclamen coum,* which has grown into a large patch. After *C. coum* slips into dormancy in March, it is replaced by a nasturtium from the dry Chilean Andes Mountains. *Tropaeolum polyphyllum* emerges with wandering shoots of silver-blue, lobed leaves. Countless yellow nasturtium flowers are held in its leaf axils. It drapes itself among and over yuccas and agaves for a long season in late spring and summer. Its tubers burrow deep into the soil, at least 3 to 4 feet, which we learned when we tried to propagate it for nursery sale. When grown as seedlings in an old wine half-barrel, its tubers moved to the bottom within two years. It only thrives in poor summer dry ground. In perennial borders, it withers away. By midsummer, seedlings of the California poppy in many colors and blue nigella have taken over the same area in the garden.

Triteleia ixioides 'Starlight' with *Allium schubertii* in the lower right.

Cyclamen coum in bloom.

Tropaeolum polyphyllum flowering after *Cyclamen coum* in the same space.

Blue *Triteleia laxa* Queen Fabiola with blue flowers joined by California poppies (*Eschscholzia californica*), both native to the West Coast (California and Oregon).

Firecracker flower, *Dichelostemma ida-maia,* is also a West Coast native.

With spring warmth, yellow *Triteleia ixioides* emerges, along with very pale *T. ixioides* 'Starlight', blue brodiaeas, and brilliant red and yellow *Dichelostemma ida-maia* (firecracker flower) on thin, wiry stems. Bulbs such as the latter three look awkward on their own and are best grown among and through grasses and low shrubs as you often find them in the wild. Many western native bulbs are long and thin-legged to compete with other vegetation trying to reach the light, almost vine-like.

Majestic desert candles (*Eremurus* spp.) from western Asia were an early acquisition. Some colors were devoured within a couple of years, while some, especially the white statuesque *E. himalaicus* and the later flowering *E. bungei*, were never touched and have multiplied over the years with tall wands of sweet-smelling flower racemes. Being a desert dweller, their emerging strap-like leaf rosettes need sunlight to flower well. We grow many in a spreading carpet of silver zauschneria, dormant in winter, and the suckering *Phlomis italica* with soft, woolly, lance-shaped leaves. These we cut to the ground each winter so the eremurus leaves are exposed to light. Planted in a dense perennial border they lose vigor and stop blooming, but here among yuccas, manzanitas, and airy grasses, such as *Stipa tenuissima*, they thrive and multiply. We leave the tall, decorative seed heads until they spill their seed. The Mexican feather grass (*Stipa tenuissima*) reseeds prolifically, and in some regions of the country is considered an invasive, but in our garden, it

Mexican feather grass
(*Stipa tenuissima*, syn.
Nassella tenuissima) and
Dichelostemma ida-maia
'Pink Diamond'.

seems that only a few of the many seedlings actually mature. It gives an airy, natural feel to the garden with its 2-foot blond seed stems swaying at the faintest touch of wind. If there is too much somewhere, it is easily taken out without need for a weeding tool.

Tall, narrow, feathered plumes blowing in the breeze is the best way I can describe *Stipa barbata*, a singular grass. Each seed carries an awn at its tip with an augur-like appendage, ending in 10 inches of a narrow tail, fringed with fine hairs, luminous in sunlight. The fringed appendage serves to carry it away with the wind. The auger-like drill at the seed tip anchors it in the soil, or in the sock of the unwary visitor. It only thrives in full sun and dry soil and has never been invasive for us.

A dry garden is not complete without alliums, with straw-colored, symmetrical spheres that last long past flowering. *Allium schubertii*, at most 2 feet tall with a 1- to 2-foot umbel of violet, starry flowers of unequal length, has the look of a fireworks show. Dramatically displayed in a low ground cover of mountain buckwheat, or zauschneria, it will not be overlooked. Like the western tumbleweed, its head will eventually break off its stem and roll in the wind to site itself decoratively in another corner, presumably to distribute its seeds, though sadly we have not come across its seedlings in our garden. Other fireworks on a smaller scale, summer-blooming *Allium carinatum* subsp. *pulchellum* in white

Summertime in the chaparral garden, with California poppies (*Eschscholzia californica*) and silver-leaved *Brachyglottis greyi.*

Stipa barbata (feather grass) with *Callistemon* 'Woodlander's Red' as backdrop.

Silver *Eryngium maritimum.*

Euphorbia rigida.

or purple, makes a great companion to airy grasses or spreading through the many penstemons and sedums at this site.

More shrubs fill empty niches, the taller ones used as backdrop along the open fence- fronting meadow and forest. From Italy came the fragrant 10-foot-tall, gangly, Mount Aetna broom (*Genista aetnensis*) and from California, white-flowered *Carpenteria californica*, which likes a bit of extra food in our soil to keep its leaves a glossy dark green. Here, we mix big, bold dryland sedges and the never-thirsty, always presentable evergreen *Euphorbia characias* subsp. *wulfenii*. We remove some of the euphorbias that grow tired and age after a few years, leaving the best seedlings behind. For such a drought-tolerant plant, I am astounded how easily they can be pulled.

Golden sumac (*Rhus typhina* 'Tiger Eyes') dominates the end of the path, framed by a blue *Cupressus arizonica* and a host of flowering sedums, penstemons, and euphorbias.

A viewing bench at the edge of the gravel garden strategically placed in the shade under a weeping Douglas fir (*Pseudotsuga menziesii* 'Graceful Grace') looks down the center path. Framed by a blue weeping *Cupressus arizonica*, the end of the path is dominated by glowing yellow *Rhus typhina* 'Tiger Eyes' (golden sumac). Radiant yellow turns to shades of orange and red in fall, equally eye-catching. Yes, it suckers as all sumacs do, but in this case it is an advantage since it grows equally well in rich or poor soil, sun or light shade; I have seen it used in sidewalk plantings, perennial gardens, or as a striking contrast to conifers. Careful pruning (don't leave stubs) can keep it to desired height and width.

A rich plant community surrounds the sumac: powder-blue perovskia, silvery, red-flowered *Zauschneria septentrionalis* 'Select *Mattole*', creeping

Zauschneria septentrionale 'Select Mattole'.

Digitalis 'Honey Trumpet'.

Opuntia polyacantha ×macrorhiza, even self-sown *Helleborus ×sternii*. Often, a golden-feathered sumac may sprout among them. If it threatens to smother them, it is easily pulled, and a new sucker, perhaps in a better spot, will replace it.

Growing here is one foxglove that doesn't reseed and I wish it would. A hybrid discovered by Xera Nursery in a batch of seedlings, *Digitalis* 'Honey Trumpet' is a truly perennial treasure, with copper-orange flowers, reblooming all summer in part shade. It only thrives for us in the sandy gravel of this part of the garden. In rich soil, it becomes a biennial.

We experimented with more shrubs among the conifers and lower perennials. We found a *Berberis thunbergii* seedling in one of our gravel paths as a little promising orphan, probably an offspring of *B. thunbergii* 'Aurea' and *B. thunbergii* 'Rose Glow'. Now named 'Tangelo' in the trade, its colors change throughout the seasons from copper-red tipped in spring, through summer as chartreuse with black-red, dipped-in-ink tips into fall as a stunning crimson, rivaling the burning bush of ancient scripture. The depth of its leaf color is much more vibrant in hot, impoverished, dry ground than spoiled in compost-laden soil in a mixed border.

Another unlikely contender was *Daphne ×transatlantica* 'Eternal Fragrance', not a shrub one would generally think of as a chaparral plant. These have integrated well among penstemons, grasses, and other happy intruders such as *Helleborus foetidus* and *H. ×sternii*, all from dry, rocky, southern Europe.

After years of planting, we delight in our successes and have learned from our failures. We now enjoy a garden that was planned but became its own mini

Daphne ×transatlantica 'Eternal Fragrance'.　　　*Penstemon heterophyllus* 'Electric Blue'.

biome. For example, *Crocosmia* 'Star of the East' settled itself in the midst of *Muhlenbergia rigens* and *Yucca filamentosa* 'Variegata' behind dark-flowered sedums and opuntia cactus. In this hot, arid environment it assumed a shorter, sturdier stature. I still don't know how the crocosmias settled here, and I could not have designed it better.

Several years ago we planted a group of compact *Helleborus ×sternii* and silver forms of *H. foetidus* here in full sun with little water as a trial to see how they would fare. They seeded themselves happily among grasses and pines. Purple winecup, *Callirhoe involucrata*, draped itself over their foliage in spots, and *Penstemon heterophyllus* 'Electric Blue' and others became their neighbors. In the wild these plants would have been growing continents apart, but their shared love for heat and drought brings them together here in common, shared growing conditions.

August through fall is the season of flowering sedums. With flowers from blond to pink to dark purple, all seeded themselves from just a few bought years ago. Visited by myriad bees they are intent on creating yet more seedlings and have invaded neighboring beds. *Penstemon ×mexicali* in pink, also a prolific reseeder in this area, makes a great combination. But, "Best of Show in June" are undoubtedly the prolific California poppies (*Eschscholzia californica*), all originally from a packet of 'Thai Silk' seed mix. From deep, wine red, dark orange, pink, to white, often with fluted petals and a silky, chiffon-like texture, these color forms are rarely found in the wild where yellow or orange predominate. At the end of their first June bloom, we pull out the more common yellow or orange

Sempervivums and
Tropaeolum polyphyllum.

and those that crowd smaller vegetation. Then we cut the rest back hard for a second, more modest bloom later in summer. We collect seed from favorites to sprinkle over the gravel for next year's bloom.

In a moister spot on the very slight downhill slope, backed by *Rhamnus frangula* 'Fine Line' and an August-flowering blue *Vitex agnus-castus*, we planted a collection of colorful garden hybrid penstemons among grasses, sedums, prickly, pale yellow *Argemone mexicana,* and the ever-present *Helleborus foetidus*. The penstemons are longer lived, more compact, and showier planted here than in a crowded perennial border.

We collected seed and cuttings in the Cascade Mountains from *Eriogonum umbellatum* (sulfur flower or mountain buckwheat) and *Eriophyllum lanatum*

California poppies
(*Eschscholzia californica*)
from 'Thai Silk' mix.

(Oregon sunshine). Both have formed low carpets slowly but steadily and are long-lived perennials. The Oregon sunshine, with bright yellow spring daisies and silver leaves, is never as tight a cushion as in its mountain home, but more of a lax carpet here in the valley though densely flowered. The mountain buckwheat, that languishes in richer, damper soil, has become one of our oldest inhabitants, the first seedlings we grew for this gravel dryland. In spring, they are covered in sulfurous yellow umbels, turning bronzy as they mature.

In our initial enthusiasm, we asked our famed friend, Panayoti Kelaidis, then curator of the Alpine Garden at Denver Botanic Gardens, for a bit of eriogonum seed from different species and locations because they were doing so well for us. About a pound of seed arrived in the mail, enough to supply acres. Such is the generosity of gardeners.

We collected seed of another mountain buckwheat in Oregon near the border of Crater Lake National Park at an elevation of about 5000 feet. It loves crawling over broken cement blocks and gravel and has formed a carpet of intense silver covered with the same sulfur flowers in spring. Carpets of matt-forming rosettes of sempervivums in green or red, some with spiderweb-like filaments, flow over the edge of pathways among small rocks and the old broken cement, and are good neighbors for eriogonums.

Although yuccas are spiky and unfriendly to the weeder, they are dramatic foliage accents and too beautiful to omit in this site. We had to incorporate them for that perennial vertical accent and foliage contrast. *Yucca rostrata* 'Sapphire Skies', much hardier than we assumed, grows to small tree-like proportions, a shimmering blue ball of a thousand swords. Old leaves will droop, turn brown,

and cling to the trunk. We leave them as frost protection. A sudden cold snap of –10°F in December 2013, which killed trees and also a giant, 8-foot *Yucca schottii*, left *Yucca rostrata* untouched but for some brown tips on the leaves.

Low-growing *Yucca filamentosa*, *Y. gloriosa*, and *Y. pallida* sometimes develop black fungus spots on older foliage in particularly wet spring weather. Those leaves can be pruned off, or if really unsightly the whole plant can be cut back. After we have done that with the variegated *Yucca gloriosa*, a whole forest of new fresh shoots will arise, growing to over a foot in height the first year.

I had never been successful growing the southeastern native butterfly weed, *Asclepias tuberosa*, in amended soil, but here in dry sandy silt and full sun, the 4-inch pots grew within three years into shrub-like proportions—3 feet tall, long-lived perennials covered with many-flowered cymes of orange or yellow flowers. This milkweed species feels at home here with conifers and grasses. Black-striped tiger swallowtail butterflies flock to sip their nectar. On rare occasions we spot a bright orange monarch butterfly. We hope to attract more by growing another one of their favorite flowers, *Asclepias speciosa*, the

Yucca rostrata 'Sapphire Skies' and Salvia microphylla.

^ *Salvia microphylla* 'Hot Lips' with *Yucca filamentosa* 'Variegata' and *Verbascum bombyciferum*.
⌃ *Asclepias speciosa* flowers are very fragrant.

^ *Asclepias tuberosa* with swallowtail butterfly.
⌃ *Asclepias speciosa* with monarch butterfly caterpillars.

showy milkweed, or silkweed, well deserving of its name. Three-foot stems, clothed in silver-felted leaves, move along by underground rhizomes and can increase with time into quite a patch of plants, easy to control if space is a concern. Their flowering cymes, 4- to 5-inch balls of pink, starry clusters, appear in early summer deliciously scented and beautiful when examined at close range. Stop and take a whiff. Each year I hope the rare monarch butterflies will lay eggs on the leaves for future generations. Large, decorative, spindle-shaped seed heads burst in fall, packed with seeds wrapped in silk. When dry, the seeds will float away in the wind on silky strands.

Here in the chaparral garden, and only here, *Salvia microphylla* has become the glorious perennial shrub it is meant to be. In this harsh environment it has proven hardy to the occasional 0°F freeze. The tiny 4-inch starts have

> *Asclepias tuberosa*.

Leaves of a first-year rosette of *Verbascum bombiciferum* 'Arctic Summer'.

Amaryllis belladonna

become 3 ½-by-6-foot shrubs, with myriad bright red flowers. In the case of 'Hot Lips' the upper hooded lip is white in stark contrast to the crimson 'hot' lower lip. Blooming from late June to frost, they act as battleground for the rufous hummingbirds and as magnets to all sorts of insects—a visual as well as a sipping feast.

Self-sown verbascums supply the narrow upright punctuation that keeps a planting like this from losing form and definition. *Verbascum chaixii* bears slender flower panicles to 3 feet in either white or yellow with mauve centers. They bloom for a long time during summer but should be thinned. Their basal leaves are large and can cover up a smaller plant. It is good to check now and then to see what's under there, especially in a dense planting. I let plants go to seed in only a few strategic spots. They are prolific self-sowers, but I wouldn't be without them.

More impressive is *Verbascum bombyciferum* 'Arctic Summer', sporting huge, soft leaves of silver velvet that invite stroking. In its second year, 8-foot, white, woolly, branched spikes are carrying myriad sulphur-yellow flowers that assume grotesque, ghost-like shapes of arms and tentacles spreading in all directions as the seasons progress and flowers go to seed. Tall grasses in our wet winters mold and collapse, draping other plants with their sad remains, but the twisted arms of 'Artic Summer' appear frozen in spectral contortions that bring life and interest to the winter garden.

Cyclamen graecum, with foliage beautifully marked in silver and no two plants with the same pattern, only thrives for us here in the dry gravel soil. It

Yucca rostrata 'Sapphire Skies' and the fall silhouette of *Verbascum bombyciferum* 'Polar Summer'.

buries its corms deeper than other cyclamens, increasing its hardiness. It arises in late summer with soft rose flowers, shaded somewhat by the tall *Asclepias speciosa*. How excited we were to discover it one October with manifold silver leaf variations, growing in an old olive orchard in the Peleponnese region of Greece. For the sheer wonder and beauty of it, we decorated a large rock with a collage of leaves from many different plants, leaving it for the farmer to find and wonder.

In 1989, Ernie and I, as new members of Hardy Plant Society of Oregon (HPSO), went to our first exciting study weekend in Lincoln City, Oregon. Of course, we purchased plants from the many vendors to fill our empty garden spaces. We bought one plant of *Hibiscus trionum,* a half-hardy little perennial. In our chaparral garden, it displays open, creamy flowers with dark brown centers from summer through fall. It faithfully reseeds in gravelly, dry spots. It has been with us for over thirty years, longer than many trees, and is always pretty, never overly aggressive.

Late summer also brings the naked ladies (*Amaryllis belladonna*) with their impressive pink flowers on bare stems and the yellow fall crocus, *Sternbergia lutea*. Both species need dry summer dormancy. Naked ladies make great companions for blue, late-blooming lilies of the Nile (*Agapanthus* sp.).

the
conifer
and heather
garden

IN THE EARLY 1980s Ernie fell in love with conifers and joined the American Conifer Society. Conifers are a guy thing. After learning all specifics on coniferous genera—species, cultivars, needle count, cone size and shape—Ernie declared that we must have an arboretum of some of the most garden-worthy selections. The added benefits would be that this part of the ever-increasing garden acreage would require little water and be practically maintenance free—the magic words. We live on our now 50-acre farm (we had sold 20 acres in 1977 to pay off the mortgage), with an ever-present temptation to increase garden space, just a little bit, and a bit more, to the point of our utter exhaustion.

We had not come to that point yet, however, so the meadow adjacent to the rock garden was turned into a conifer arboretum. Here the male element predominates. We killed the grass, tilled the whole area, about ⅛ acre, and mulched it with bark chips. We planted conifers, carefully distanced from each other according to the labels' "ultimate size" descriptions. However, the female element, namely I, was not satisfied. It was a museum-like collection—solid, labeled, anchored—each one in its

< *Chamaecyparis lawsoniana* 'Filiformis' is pruned yearly as a topiary tree, an important conifer component that is a focal point in our design.

The beginnings of the conifer garden collection in the early 1980s.

own universe like people waiting at a bus stop. We decided that, at the very least, we needed winding paths between the various geometric shapes to bring some fluidity to the area.

Enticing spaces between the bare, mulched spots invited more greenery. What plants partner well with conifers connecting one tree or shrub with the other? In other words, how do we make a collection into a garden? This area abuts the rockery to the south, forming a backdrop where garden meets meadow and trees. A distant fence on the south side, not visible from the garden, keeps the deer at bay. *Cornus sanguinea* 'Midwinter Fire' placed at irregular intervals between conifers and wild meadow is now the defining border between our gardening ambitions and the tree-studded meadow beyond.

In sunny spots and at the edges of the new paths, we planted feathery heaths and heathers, *Calluna* and *Erica*, with needle-like foliage. Grasses and kniphofias planted in between acted as upright, yet lax, elements with soft texture and movement. All the heaths and heathers are shorn into an undulating wave of green, gold, and gray. It is important to shear right after flowering, which can be almost any time of the year, depending on the species or cultivar. They are never pruned all at the same time. With yearly shearing, heathers can be very long-lived in well-drained, moist ground. Another sheared component in our garden, our topiary tree, *Chamaecyparis lawsoniana* 'Filiformis', acts as a focal point.

As we turn west toward our country road, the ground descends slightly to the road, resulting in a moving but very high water table in winter. Even in our rainless summers, the grass in this meadow never turns brown. Sheets of 3-foot

Camassia leichtlinii.

Helleborus foetidus 'Red Silver' in a dry spot at the base of a dwarf cedar of Lebanon.

tall, blue *Camassia leichtlinii* subsp. *leichtlinii*, greater camas, a bulb of wet western meadows, grow and increase here in this moist spot at a rapid rate. They bloom and seed with abandon. Caution is advised: it is best to plant this where it has generous space to multiply. This area has also proven to be a happy environment for some very handsome moisture-loving conifers.

Twenty-five or more years later, little is left of the original planting. There were conifers too exuberant in growth, changing light to shade around them. Their fast growth led to breaking up in beautiful but deadly ice rains, their branches adorned with ice crystals the weight of chandeliers. Heavy, windy rainstorms upended some and a record early freeze killed two weeping giant sequoias (*Sequoiadendron giganteum* 'Pendulum') and a large Italian cypress. Every loss can be turned into a gain. With more knowledge of our soil and surroundings, we learned to plant a new shrub or tree even more beautiful.

Thirty years ago, J. C. Raulston, late director of the Arboretum at North Carolina State University, gave us a gallon-size *Pinus taeda* 'Nana'. In Oregon it grew at twice the speed of its eastern counterparts. Each year I climbed its branches way beyond ten-foot ladder height, to prune and thin its branches; I was surprised at my daring. It became the center of the so-called conifer garden, a magnificent though shade-spreading tree. Then, in 2013, came the early freeze of -10°F, followed two months later by very heavy, wet snow. The pine, already damaged by the freeze, was a pitiful wreck of broken limbs, so we were forced to cut it down. Although we were dejected to lose the sentimental connection to a valued friend who died an early death, the sun returned where shade had been.

Rock garden with conifers as a backdrop.

The center of the conifer garden.

The view to the meadow beyond, planted earlier to oaks and swamp cypress, opened a new vista. The garden seemed bigger with the return of the view to the beyond. New challenges and opportunities offered themselves. The golden lodgepole pine (*Pinus contorta* 'Chief Joseph'), green all summer, which magically changes to glowing gold with winter's cold, became visible again from our patio and window.

The so-called conifer garden has slowly transformed into an area of trees, shrubs, and perennials appropriate for our climate and sandy soil. Some species, such as the Colorado blue spruce (*Picea pungens*) and its dwarf cultivars, are only desirable here in their youth. With our mild, wet winters they do not shed their brown, dead needles of previous years, looking uglier as they advance in age. They belong to windblown, sunny, snowy mountains. Other species, mostly dense globose balls such as *Cryptomeria japonica* 'Globosa', turned into bigger balls. And what was a cute little plant in a pot became a dull adult in the ground. So, it was again, "Off with their heads." A gardener is, after all, supreme judge when it comes to life and death in a garden.

The conifer survivors of the initial planting have become an integral part of the garden. There is no more conifer collection. *Pinus longaeva* at the edge of the rockery in mean, lean, sandy grit has grown into a 12-foot narrow beauty, needing another thousand or more years to bristlecone pine maturity. The small Hinoki cypresses, such as *Chamaecyparis obtusa* 'Hage', 'Rigid Dwarf', and 'Nana', and selected small mugo pines have become longstanding favorites. Imitating ancient trees, especially with a bit of annual thinning and pruning, their truly dwarf dimensions will suggest an alpine landscape when paired with low carpets of dianthus and other miniature spreaders beneath. The best selection of truly dwarf mugo pines can be found in large nurseries among the blocs of their seedling grown plants. Those with the shortest annual growth and needles, no more than an inch, can become long-loved alpine garden inhabitants with a bit of shaping.

At the eastern end of the original conifer collection, a solitary, slender, 20-foot *Cryptomeria japonica* 'Sekkan-sugi' holds its pendulous branches, with billows of golden tips, against the sky. This was also a tiny plant in a 4-inch pot when we innocents bought it so many years ago as a truly dwarf tree, but we don't regret the purchase.

A tree with swaying glaucous manes on weeping, far-flung branches is how I would describe one of my favorite junipers. *Juniperus scopulorum* 'Tolleson's Weeping' has grace and elegance and loves our sandy environment. After a precarious beginning—it almost fell over in a windy, wet winter and had to be sturdily staked—it grew large and wide. Its branches harbor shrubs such as *Calycanthus ×raulstonii* 'Hartlage Wine' and *Berberis thunbergii* f. *atropurpurea* 'Helmond Pillar', with a crowd of stately *Helleborus argutifolius* and creeping *Euphorbia amygdaloides* var. *robbiae* in its shady understory.

The huge aspen behind the juniper looks as if it is about to shower silver nuggets from above with the slightest breeze. Living in a valley south of a large reservoir, soft summer breezes from the north often blow our way, which are much appreciated. The leaves play with light and shade, constantly creating subtle new patterns of light and color and making a delightful shushing sound when the breeze picks up. *Cupressus arizonica* var. *glabra* 'Blue Ice', displaying dense sprays of powder blue scaly leaves, is happiest in parched soil at the edge of our plantings. We pruned the lower branches as it grew skyward to expose the smooth, exfoliating red bark.

Buxus sempervirens 'Graham Blandy', a narrow, upright growing cultivar.

We have, by now, planted six golden Chinese dawn redwoods, *Metasequoia glyptostroboides* 'Gold Rush', the two oldest living in constantly moist ground. What a glow. Like larches, they are deciduous and turn bronze in fall before losing their needles. Fast growers, they develop a slightly buttressed trunk with age that is much fissured above and handsome to behold.

Last but not least of our moisture-loving conifers is the aptly named swamp cypress, *Taxodium distichum*, also called bald cypress. We first came across it in winter at a wholesale nursery, whose employee assumed they were dead since their branches were bare at that time of year. Even though they come from the swamps of the southeastern United States, they are bone hardy and put on their new growth in spring quite late. The new foliage is never frosted, unlike the Japanese larch (*Larix kaempferi*), another deciduous conifer, which often sprouts its first green shoots when spring frosts are still prevalent, and new growth is browned.

In some winters, if wet, heavy snow, or ice rain, collects on bare branches of the bald cypress still covered in places with last year's clumps of dead needles stuck on crossed twigs, a limb may break, but verdant new growth will cover the scars, giving the tree a somewhat aged, ragged, but not unpleasant appearance. Ours are slowly developing small 'knees', aerial root bumps formed away from the trunk. The fall color is a marvelous bronzy brown lasting for a long time,

Giant fennel, from Greece (*Ferula communis*), in bloom with *Juniperus scopulorum* 'Tolleson's Weeping' in the background.

Species tree peony *Paeonia delavayi*.

Paeonia 'A la Mode'.

Fritillaria imperialis at the foot of a weeping Norway spruce, *Picea nigra* 'Pendula'.

> Heathers and hardy banana (*Musa basjoo*) with *Calycanthus* ×*raulstonii* 'Hartlage Wine'.

glowing in the autumnal sunlight. In the Pacific Northwest, the variety *Taxodium distichum* var. *imbricatum* (also known as *T. ascendens* 'Nutans') seems less hardy, ours sporting many dead branches among new sprouting green. This tree may be better suited to an urban, or more protected, environment.

With the large *Pinus taeda* 'Nana' gone, dwarf shrubs in the alpine garden are sunlit again, the colors changing throughout the seasons and visible from our patio to the north. Small shrubs are punctuated by tall, narrow *Buxus sempervirens* 'Graham Blandy'. A weeping, 6-foot Norway spruce (*Picea nigra* 'Pendula') is dwarfed by statuesque, lacy-foliaged giant fennel (*Ferula communis*) grown from seed collected in a Greek meadow. Tree peonies, gloriously flowered red and yellow in spring, with bold, dissected leaves that turn golden and orange in fall, are interspersed with weeping mounds of deodar cedars from the original conifer collection.

Yellow- and red-leaved cultivars of *Berberis thunbergii* provide color spots among conifers. A big clump of *Crocosmia* ×*crocosmiiflora* 'Emily McKenzie' throws up its bright orange and black flowers in August, but is dormant in spring when the same spot is inhabited by lusty Dutch hyacinths showing off their colors. The silver-flecked foliage of 'Winter Moonbeam' hellebore doesn't mind being shaded temporarily during summer by a self-sown blue geranium and the crocosmias. *Kniphofia caulescens* repeats the same shade of orange in its flowers in the next bed, where earlier, showy *Paeonia* 'Bartzella' bloomed in yellow.

A spring bed of Dutch hyacinths and *Helleborus* ×*sternii*.

Poncirus trifoliata 'Flying Dragon', with needle-like thorns.

A visitor reclining on the patio looks upon this view, bordered by taller shrubs. To the left, giant green leaves of *Musa basjoo* sway and clatter in the breeze. It is a 12-foot hardy banana with inedible hard fruit, and next to it, a most viciously spiny shrub with equally inedible citrus fruit. *Poncirus trifoliata* 'Flying Dragon', from Korea, has twisty branches, which are deadly to prune, but its white flowers and orange fruit are beautiful to behold beneath the impressive swaying leaves of the banana. In winter, the banana leaves will turn brown and decay. The whole trunk may even collapse in severe winters (0 to −10°F), reappearing each April with new growth, even if frozen to the ground.

More shrubbery crowds together behind heathers, eucomis, and blue Nile lilies. A handsome threesome, made up of *Berberis jamesiana* from China, with winter red fruit shaped like jeweled teardrops, lavender rose of Sharon (*Hibiscus syriacus*) from India, and *Hydrangea paniculata* 'Fire and Ice', the parents found in many parts of Asia, are backed by the hulking South American giant feathered Pampas grass (*Cortaderia selloana* 'Pumila'). And behind them stands a handsome, slender, silver-needled *Pinus koraiensis*, aptly named 'Silver Ray', from Korea, surrounded by Joe Pye weed (*Eupatorium purpureum*) from the United States.

Hydrangea paniculata 'Fire and Ice' and *Eupatorium purpureum*, Joe Pye weed.

We turn from silver to gold, with yellow-foliaged *Cornus alba* 'Aurea' from Europe, *Leycesteria formosa* 'Golden Lanterns' from Asia, and *Corylopsis spicata* 'Aurea' from Japan duking it out behind green heathers. A twisted, dark green hemlock (*Tsuga diversifolia*), also from Japan, and the almost black-leaved *Weigela florida* 'Wine and Roses' from Asia, bring more subdued color to the scene. *Cornus alba* 'Elegantissima' in front of the hemlock is one of my favorite shrubs, with green, cleanly white-edged foliage and winter red stems.

On reading this, you might say, "What a cacophony of color, leaf, and needle, from a banana to a heather-bun and beyond," but strangely it all works well together. Harmonious chaos is possible in a garden, with denizens from multitudes of countries of origin. Would that we humans could be as comradely as is the diverse plant world here represented.

the glory
of the
autumn
and winter
garden

FALL IS A study in contrasts. The days shorten and only during this season do the spotted towhees sing their song of two melancholy notes that sound like *good-byeee*! And yet, both spring and fall begin and end the seasons of growth in a blaze of color. In our valley, leaves start to color toward the second half of October. In our garden, with trees and shrubs from regions around the world, the show can last to the latter part of November unless a harsh frost browns the foliage with sudden cold and sends crisp, curled, tawny leaves sailing earthward.

As the garden has grown older and larger, our once small trees, selected for fall color, have matured. Bold and subtle colors, dark and bright hues play off each other. Even the browned leaves of a red oak and the dark crimson-black of *Berberis thunbergii* f. *atropurpurea* 'Helmond Pillar' act their parts in the interplay of color. The emerald backdrop of conifers enriches the golds and orange-reds of the deciduous shrubs and trees. Visually, I find this mix very satisfying, like covering a green Christmas tree with colorful ornaments. When the dance of many-colored autumn leaves is done, we are not left solely with bare branches of dormant trees against the gray

< The conifer garden view toward the west with deciduous *Metasequoia glyptostroboides* 'Gold Rush' now turning bronze before needles drop.

skies of winter. The green and blue of conifers—fir, pine, cypress, and spruce—accompany us throughout fall and winter, when they are refreshed by rain and cleansed by wind, shedding their spent needles to mulch the soil.

Nothing compares with the sudden transformation of an ordinary green lodgepole pine into a gloriously golden-needled conifer. *Pinus contorta* 'Chief Joseph' does just that. Named after Chief Joseph (1840–1904) of the Wallowa Valley Nez Perce tribe, this brilliantly colored tree was found in the Wallowa Mountains of eastern Oregon by plantsman Doug Will on a fall hunting trip. He supposedly dug it up with an axe and brought the treasure back to Sandy, Oregon. Imagine his surprise when, with the return of warm weather in spring,

A spotted towhee singing a melancholy *good-bye.*

his brilliant golden pine turned green. Our 'Chief Joseph' has slowly grown to a height of 20 feet and delights us every fall and winter when it takes center stage and glows like gold under gray and foggy skies. It is difficult to graft and so it is expensive to purchase, but don't let that deter you. It is worth it.

Deciduous conifers, such as bald cypress (*Taxodium* spp.), larch (*Larix* spp.), and dawn redwood (*Metasequoia glyptostroboides*) join the fall parade of color with yellow, bronze-red, and brown foliage before dropping their needles. These trees renew themselves each spring with fresh new growth shoots of delicious lime-green. In fall three dwarf larches of twisted and spreading growth (*Larix decidua* 'Little Bogle', *L. kaempferi* 'Haverbeck', and *L. laricina* 'Nana')

Fall scene in the conifer garden with blue *Abies procera* 'Glauca Prostrata', *Berberis thunbergii* f. *atropurpurea* 'Royal Cloak', and yellow tupelo, *Nyssa sylvatica*.

Oxydendrum arboreum, the small sourwood tree, turns a crimson-red in fall at our back door.

Ginkgo tree (*Ginkgo biloba*) showering ducats of gold.

form a golden triangle by our entrance among a host of colorful small shrubs and perennials and one small crimson-red sourwood (*Oxydendrum arboreum*) which, in fall, is the same color as the bright red back door.

In the perennial garden, *Parrotia persica* 'Vanessa', a narrower form of the normally wide-branched ironwood species, and *Nyssa sylvatica* 'Autumn Cascades', a weeping member of the usually broadly conical black gum (*Nyssa sylvatica*), grow close together. Both are clothed in warm yellow, orange, and red autumn foliage. At a distance southward, our oldest, tall, upright tupelo (*N. sylvatica*), in full red fall dress, is sited with *Cupressus arizonica* var. *glabra* 'Blue Ice' as an effective blue backdrop. Beneath them, *Berberis thunbergii* 'Tangelo', with leaves of fiery reds, purples, green-yellows all on the same plants, changes colors day to day like an overstimulated chameleon. A crooked-trunked ginkgo tree, bought long ago as a variegated shrub that reverted back to green, turns to a rich yellow overnight and, just as suddenly, showers ducats of gold and then stands bare in a carpet of leafy riches.

Winter golden *Pinus contorta* 'Chief Joseph' seen from under *Ulmus ×hollandica* 'Jacqueline Hillier'.

Stewartia koreana, *S. malacodendron,* and *S. sinensis* were originally planted in the perennial garden, as well as other well-watered garden spots, for their beautiful peeling bark and camellia-like flower display. With advancing age, their fall colors have taken on vivid reds. They are slow to grow, with a broadly columnar shape, which for many small gardens is a definite plus.

With small gardens in mind, I must mention the limitless choice of small Japanese maples. Walking through a nursery specializing in Japanese maples during the fall season opens the heart to limitless desire, but not to limitless space or pocketbook. Most Japanese maples will suit the gardener of a small city lot, and often even the cheaper seedling maples will provide glorious autumn color of reds, purples, and yellows. Our best-loved Japanese maple for its splendid fall color came to us as a landscaping giveaway. It was a sad-looking veteran of botched prunings, or, more accurately, choppings, to its top and took many years to recover with gentle shaping and thinning. We just knew it carried good genes in that formerly misshapen trunk. Now, in early fall, all its tips turn a fiery red and slowly a multicolored splendor of orange, yellow, and reds transforms

Aralia elata foliage in fall.

the lower leaves. Growing in the center of our patio, it greets us upon awakening, outside the glass doors of our bedroom. It extends its red tips above the roof to thrill Ernie in the office as he sits at the computer.

Acer japonicum 'Aconitifolium', a compact multibranched erect maple, is worth growing for its fan-like, deeply dissected leaves alone, but come fall the whole tree turns flaming crimson-red with purple touches. Ours grow in light shade under a tall redwood and Norway spruce, but their brilliance of color is not diminished and lasts for a long time.

The latest Japanese maple to color for us is the narrow, densely branched 'Shishigashira' (*Acer palmatum* 'Shishigashira'). It changes from green to subtle rust colors, which we love. It is a favorite with the red-crowned kinglet vireos, which visit every morning to pick aphid eggs or other minute insect life from its curling leaves and congested branches.

One of the earliest shrubs to announce the fall season is the tall *Fothergilla major*, covered in spring with white bottlebrush flowers. In fall its deep yellow foliage offers bright contrast to the deep purple-red *Acer palmatum*

'Scolopendrifolium' growing next to it in semi-shade. Small *Fothergilla gardenii* 'Jane Platt' explodes into fireworks of reds, oranges, and yellows while the cultivar 'Blue Shadow', most handsome with blue foliage in summer, turns deep red in fall. Our fothergillas do equally well in light shade or full sun and are adaptable to dry sites under trees.

Upright and covered in fall with golden yellow foliage, *Corylopsis platypetala* grows against the northeast corner of our house. *Corylopsis* is a genus I would not do without. Early racemes of hanging yellow spring flowers on bare branches give way to pleated leaves and colorful fall foliage in shades of pleasing yellow. Corylopsis is easy to shape and thin by pruning, looking beautiful with a carpet of hellebores underneath whose flowering time coincides with their own.

Calycanthus ×raulstonii 'Hartlage Wine', covered in red flowers all summer, took us by surprise. Its large leaves turned rich Irish butter yellow this past fall. Draped with blue tendrils of weeping *Juniperus scopulorum* 'Tolleson's Weeping' from above, it makes for a very showy fall combination.

Euonymus alatus 'Monstrosa', with bizarre, corky wings on its branches and dangling orange-red fruit, earns its common name of burning bush. Fall sets its leaves ablaze in solid crimson glory. It grows into a large spreading shrub so is best placed in the background among conifers, where its undiminished fire can be enjoyed even from the distant windows of the house. It is apparently an invasive in some areas of the eastern and southeastern United States, but not here in the Northwest.

Cotinus 'Grace', a hybrid offspring of the purple smoke tree *C. coggygria* 'Velvet Cloak', glows a purple-pink-red with translucent leaves that reflect the light in full sun. It can be left to grow into a small shrubby tree, or can be pruned yearly. We have seen the species, *C. coggygria*, in fall on sunny rocky, dry hillsides in southeast France in brilliant color. Cotinus colors best in full sun.

Spicy winter fragrance and spidery yellow or red flower clusters in January and February announce the presence of hamamelis, the witch hazel, the earliest shrub to flower. Come fall, we can bask again in the warm glow of rich yellow- and orange-colored leaves of the many cultivars of this ever-popular shrub. The best for autumn color of all witch hazels I have seen and grown is the deep red, fragrant-flowered *Hamamelis ×intermedia* 'Diane', each leaf streaked and spotted in warm tones of yellow, red, and green, each leaf an artist's design, no two quite alike. The shrub's growth habit is more spreading than upright. We planted it underneath our living room window without inhibiting our view, tending it with just a bit of judicious pruning, of course.

The suckering shrub *Itea virginica* 'Henry's Garnet' is hardly ever seen in Northwest gardens. It is a centerpiece of our front border, visible from inside the house. Dangling racemes of white flowers cover this 3- to 4-foot shrub in spring. In full sun, leaves turn to shades of ruby- wine and orange, lasting

^ *Itea virginica* 'Henry's Garnet'.
⌃ *Hamamelis* ×*intermedia* 'Diane' in warm tones
of yellow, red, and green.
⌃ *Acer japonicum* 'Aconitifolium' turning flaming
crimson-red in fall.

^ *Hypericum* 'Kolmoran' Mystical Orange, with
clematis seed heads.
⌃ *Cornus sanguinea* 'Midwinter Fire'.

all through winter, until new spring foliage emerges. Each fall we prune the lower branches of the arching shrub to give light to *Cyclamen hederifolium*, with its marbled foliage, growing at its base. *Hydrangea quercifolia*, skirting our house and office, also hangs on to its leaves all winter. Young foliage turns a very attractive blackish red and purple in fall. As winter temperatures drop, leaves become crimson red. My favorite low-growing cultivars are 'Pee Wee' and 'Ruby Slippers', compact enough so we can look out our windows without endless pruning.

Actaea pachypoda with *Persicaria virginiana* var. *filiformis* 'Painter's Palette' (syn. *Tovara virginiana* 'Painter's Palette') make a handsome duo in the shade garden.

When frost and wind leave branches bare, the twigs, berries, and seeds take the fall show into winter. Red- and yellow-twig dogwoods (*Cornus sericea* and *C. alba*) give us a fourth season of color. Among the reds, two stand out in our garden. One of them is the older cultivar, *C. alba* 'Elegantissima', the most elegant, and so it is with gray-green leaves, margined in silver-white. Once foliage drops in late fall, its twigs glow red, reaching upward. When the winter sun hits them, they sparkle and glow. We grow them both as a suckering hedge and a single specimen so the new growth is fully visible in winter for dramatic effect. *Cornus sericea* 'Hedgerows Gold' grabs attention in summer with green-centered, golden-margined leaves and deep red, spiky branches in winter. We grew this shrub at first as a double-trunked tree until our dogs, in a nocturnal pursuit of a treed raccoon, tore all its bark off in a rage of frustration. Cut to the

< *Fothergilla major*, one of the first shrubs to color in fall.

^ Woolly caterpillar, making its regular fall appearance.
⌃ Tiny *Paris luquanensis* has showy red berries in the fall.

^ *Berberis jamesiana* with coral red fruit.
⌃ *Paris polyphylla* var. *stenophylla* bursting with plentiful berries containing seeds.

ground, it became a shrub and we now prune it regularly each spring just as new buds start showing. That way the rejuvenated shrub delights us again with fresh red growth each winter. If left unpruned, *C. alba* and *C. sericea* will grow to 12 feet and more, the larger branches losing their bright color as they age. Brightly colored prunings can be used for highly decorative late- winter arrangements, or in spring for attractive supports for early peas.

Cornus sanguinea 'Midwinter Fire' is used by us as a backdrop in full sun, visible in winter when leaves have dropped from all other shrubs. Then suddenly their spiky, yellow, orange, and red twigs brighten our southern garden border. This low-lying area tends to be very wet in winter with water often flowing aboveground. This suits moisture-loving red- and yellow- twig dogwoods just fine since riverbanks are their natural habitat.

Fall also brings to ripeness a wide variety of colorful berries. A berry's function is to spread the seed that lives inside it. Some indigestible or poisonous to us are the delight of bird or rodent, although there are reports of some introductions, such as nandina, being also poisonous to birds. But with care in our choices, it is safe for us to use them as eye candy, and therein lies the allure of decorating our winter garden with berries of bright colors. Arisaema fruits in glowing red drape over evergreen ferns long after their foliage is gone. Poisonous, white baneberry, or cohosh (*Actaea pachypoda*), with racemes of spherical berries with the odd, but somewhat appropriate, name of doll's eyes, grow among fall foliage in our woodland. Seed capsules of *Paris polyphylla* and *P. luquanensis* burst open to reveal a treasure trove of red fruits inside, long after peonies have spilled their fruits of the same color. Fascinating mushrooms spring up in woodchip-mulched paths. I am captivated by this sudden burst of fall energy and transformation of flower to fruit, of underground rhizome to spore-bearing mushroom (a fungus fruiting body).

Higher in the canopy hang the red and very sour fruits of *Cornus mas*, and little fruits of yellow and purple crabapples, which can both be used for jams

Thalictrum delavayi seed.

or jellies with lots of added sugar. Flocks of robins, undeterred by sour flavors, devour these bite-sized fruits, giving us only short glimpses of their dangling beauty. My two favorite crabapples, yellow-fruited *Malus transitoria* 'Golden Raindrops' and purple-fruited *Malus* 'Royal Raindrops', are their favorites, too. The spring beauty of their white and pink flowers lasts longer than the fruits.

Our beautiful, red-berried, *Ilex verticillata* 'Winter Red' mysteriously escapes the birds in fall. It is planted in a woodland corner near our road and overlooked by avian flocks every year. This deciduous holly has grown to enormous size, 8 feet by 10 feet, bearing an abundant, long-lasting crop of scarlet berries. I planted a small male underneath it to be sure of plentiful fruit making a wonderful show all winter unless early cold sets in and robins become very hungry.

Another shrub, the brilliantly violet-colored *Callicarpa bodinieri* var. *giraldii* 'Profusion', aptly named beautyberry, also escapes bird predation. Only when it turns so cold that it browns the berry and robins become desperate will they feed on this berry, so we get to enjoy the show of the extraordinary color often long into winter. In sun or dappled shade, it sets ample fruits hanging on its leaf axils in many-berried clusters.

People often speak of putting their garden to bed, meaning the show is over for this year, but for us the show goes on. Seed heads, berries, the winter structure of dormant trees, the greens of conifers, white trunks of aspen and birch lit up by the sun, the peeling trunks of *Acer griseum* and *Stewartia*, and even a little hellebore flower raising its bright head in December, enliven the garden and can be beautiful all year. We just have to keep our eyes and spirit open to its magic.

< View along the driveway on a foggy day in fall.

caring for the garden

I WOULD LIKE to introduce the garden's international crew, grand-sounding words for callused hands and tired backs. There is Chantal from France, with all-seeing eyes. She spots aphids and blackspot, slug and snail, and can pot and weed at astonishing speed. We would be utterly lost without her skills. There is Ernie, the only homegrown American, who can operate computer, tractor, chainsaw, chipper, and all other fearsome mechanical implements with ease, and he can fix them, too. He also loves to prune and weed. Then, there is the German of the crew, myself, trained in the German work ethic, meaning there is always more to do than you think. I am the all-around gardener.

When real high tree pruning is needed, we call on Yanis, a tree pruner from Latvia, who attacks each high climb with determination and vigor and often from the heights of a boom truck. His skilled hands and saw lighten up our woodland. Now and then, when we are in need of a strong back and mighty muscles, our neighbor, a high school teacher and coach, will recommend an eager student in need of extra cash.

< I am pruning the Bosc pear, an annual February task.

Chamaecyparis obtusa 'Crippsii' must be pruned when the golden foliage is still attractive. The pruning is half finished: the left side is unpruned.

Preparation for the new spring season in the garden starts in late October after the first frosts drive perennials into winter dormancy and trees begin to drop their leaves—the universal signal to begin fall and winter garden care. With every puff of wind, showers of gold, bronze, and red dance through the air. Leaves are settling on paths and beds. In a garden as large as ours, a blower comes in handy. It's a noisy beast, but it does the work of many rakes and we don't have close neighbors that object to the sound. The bounty of leaves after being blown into piles is carted by wheelbarrow into the vegetable garden or

used as mulch around young trees in the grassy arboretum bordering the garden. This helps to kill the grass competing for water in summer with the roots of a young tree. The dormant vegetable garden is thickly covered in leaves, which are converted to compost by summer because of the action of worms, fungi, bacteria, insects, and other arthropods. It is a miraculous transformation, repeated yearly.

We leave a thin layer of dead leaves on most shade and perennial beds, which is covered later by a layer of good, black, weed-free compost. When we spread

Branches are chipped and chips become mulch for woodland paths.

Thinning is needed in the bamboo stand. Old culms are removed in early spring before new shoots arise. New shoots are darker in color and grow very fast.

Trillium bulbs newly divided. These will go directly into the ground or be potted up for sale in early spring.

compost, we are careful not to bury the lower portions of hellebores, rhododendrons, azaleas, and other woody and evergreen plants that resent having their crowns or stems covered. On the other hand, plants that retreat underground for the winter, such as many ferns, bulbs, and herbaceous perennials, get added frost protection from a topping of compost. The many dahlia tubers even get an extra compost molehill heaped onto them that will protect them in case of a hard freeze. Paths are mulched with fresh, fragrant woodchips produced by Ernie in our woodlot with his giant chipper. All mulching is done with trusty wheelbarrow, a long but rewarding process.

Once a year, in early spring, we fertilize our bamboo hedge with a high-nitrogen grass fertilizer and thin out old culms at ground level. During a winter with a heavy snow, or even ice rain (a more common occurrence in recent years), bamboo will flatten with the weight of ice and snow. Most of it springs back once the load has melted, but some should be cut. Next year's culms will grow larger in diameter after thinning. A battery-powered reciprocating saw with a metal-cutting blade (bamboo is high in silica and hard on saw blades) makes the job fast and easy. Cut culms can be used as tree stakes, creative fencing, or trellis supports.

Fall is the best time for division of perennials, corms, and bulbs. When we cut back perennials and clematis vines at the end of the season, we have learned to leave a foot of stems and leaves aboveground, especially on plants like crocosmias, lilies, and dahlias. We try to have metal labels identifying most plants,

An ice rain is beautiful but destructive since the enormous weight of ice on branches and leaves can topple even large trees.

but these often become buried under compost, or mole and vole tunnel soil, or our heavy human foot, or simply become illegible over time.

If perennials are cut back entirely, the guessing starts: "I think this is where I had those lilies," and the spade sinks and slices the bulbs in half. Crocosmias tend to romp and need thinning each year, which is easy to accomplish with a fork as long as the stems are visible. Dahlias also divide easily at this time, and divisions for friends and plant sales can be stored dry and frost-free. Don't trust your memory; label all pots. By spring, it will be a guessing game, even for those of us who pride ourselves on our unfailing memory. Spring bulbs, rhizomes, and corms are best divided with a fork a little earlier in fall, or late summer, when dormant but still showing a little wilted top. We may mark the position of a clump of trilliums with a little bamboo stick, for example.

Alpine and chaparral plants are only mulched with gravel as the need arises, but not with rich compost, which causes extensive root rot. Early in March we fertilize all gravel-covered areas with a one-time application of either a very slow-release or pelletized organic fertilizer. At planting we incorporate a handful or more, depending on plant size, of a slow-acting organic fertilizer such as All Purpose Fish into the planting hole.

Penstemons and shrubby salvias resent fall pruning so we wait for new growth in spring before cutting them back, resisting the temptation to tidiness. As gardener, I learn not to impose my human sense of orderliness on all plant life. Shrubs with borderline hardiness are also best cut back in spring. Pruning

Ice rain has bent the
bamboo to almost ground
level. Most of it just
springs back. Only a few
culms need to be cut that
can't quite make it back
to vertical.

Often a plant has to live a while in a pot until the right spot for it can be found.

allows you to be artist in residence. It is worthwhile to learn the basics of growth habit and needs of any woody plant before you prune it. Does it flower on old or new wood (like peaches = new wood, but apples = old wood)? Does it flower on the tips of branches only, like *Hydrangea quercifolia*, or on buds of the previous year's laterals, like *Hydrangea paniculata*? Should it be pruned right after spring flowering, like the various daphnes and *Clematis sibirica* (Atragene Group), or before bud break like for fruit trees? There is also the consideration whether to thin or shear (head back) to keep the shrub in bounds, like for deutzia and weigela.

Fern pruning time is just before new fronds emerge. Old fronds have been removed.

We have learned from close observation of our plants throughout the years, and by our many mistakes. In an older garden such as ours, pruning becomes of vital importance, or only the most aggressive plants survive. As long as we want to crowd so many plants from different continents and environments together in a limited space and desire a harmonious and natural look, we need to get out sharp pruning shears, loppers, and saw.

First, stand back and ask yourself, "What form or shape would I like to see here?" For example, should I prune this shrub up, allowing for a layer of bulbs or perennials beneath it, or does it need cutting back or a thinning of its branches so the garden beyond is included and visible?

Come January, we start pruning dormant fruit trees, hazelnuts, grapes, and hardy deciduous trees and shrubs. It takes us all the way into early spring to finish. When working from a ten-foot orchard ladder or in a well-branched tree, I observe this rule: make sure to have three points of support at all times—two feet and a knee pressed against branch or ladder when using a lopper, or two feet and one hand holding on to a branch while the other is using a handsaw. I make sure my ladder is stable before climbing, and with age, I am learning not to be in a hurry and to concentrate on the job at hand.

The skeleton of deciduous trees and shrubs hidden among verdant foliage for most of the year shows to best advantage in late fall and winter, so it is the easiest time to prune. If pruned and thinned properly, winter can reveal the stark beauty of bare twisting branches and twigs. Our contorted filbert's most glorious moments come after its yearly thinning in January, its bare branches bedecked with male flowers like dangling golden ornaments.

Some vines, such as summer-blooming clematis, schizophragma, hydrangea, and, especially, wisteria, need a good cutting back. We cut all summer-blooming clematis back to near ground level to prevent them from swamping any shrub underneath and to keep those marvelous flowers at eye level.

Climbing hydrangeas on fence or trellis are cut back to keep them tight and dense, but those that climb our big, old firs and maple are allowed to romp, their twisting trunks encircling without strangling the large trees, their fragrant flowers blooming amidst tree branches.

We love our wisterias, but these need two or three prunings a year. The first wisteria that I ever planted in the early '70s, a blue-flowered *Wisteria floribunda*, invades the inside of our second-story room with snake-like tendrils if the window is left open ever so slightly. Three times a year—summer, fall, and winter—I climb the ladder and shorten the sublaterals to two buds. Six weeks later it is climbing on the roof and around the gutters. This is a vine that needs to be planted with forethought. But it's too late for us. It has climbed its way into our hearts and house.

A much more reasonable purchase for a smaller spot is the Kentucky wisteria, *Wisteria macrostachya* 'Blue Moon'. Flower racemes are a bit shorter, but incredibly abundant and fragrant, plus it reblooms reliably and plentifully. Two prunings a year will keep it in reasonable bounds. Always leave two buds on the small branches growing from the main trunk for next year's flowering.

Conifers as a group can generally be pruned in spring or fall. Among our dwarf mountain pines, we break the new candles in spring when they are soft and pliable. The little stub that is left will become the growth for that year. Especially dwarf mugo pines with a little added thinning will stay small over many years and can take on that aged look of shrubby, high-altitude conifers.

Our most ornamental ground cover, hybrid hellebores, reside now in every shady and sunny corner except the alpine and chaparral gardens. December and January are the months to cut old, weathered foliage to let new growth

Perennials held erect by gridded supports provided in April.

and blossoms shine. Old fronds on ferns are pruned only as new fronds emerge. Cutting them too early can result in severe frost damage and even kill the fern.

The latest shrubs to prune as new buds swell in March are the multicolored stems of yellow- and red-twig dogwoods, as well as *Acer circinatum* 'Pacific Fire', a vine maple with brilliant red new growth. We want to enjoy these all winter, especially when sunlight sets a sparkle upon them, so we wait to take the pruners to them until spring.

And then spring comes, verdant spring with verdant weeds. After we had done a thorough weeding, one visitor asked, hopefully, "I don't see any weeds.

What do you do?" I think she was hoping for the secret, the magic answer, which was, to her disappointment, "We weed!" Yes, we weed year in and year out, and it can become a meditative activity, spotting cardamine and oxalis hiding among the rightful inhabitants of rockery and perennial beds. A full wheelbarrow of weeds brings the day to a satisfying close, aching back notwithstanding.

Obstinate weeds masquerading as parts of choice alpines and cushion plants are dispatched with a simple and efficient tool of Ernie's devising. Take a disused handle of any tool, such as a broken shovel, for example; saw it off at about 4 to 5 inches, and drive a big 6-inch-long nail into the cut off end. Remove the head of the nail and sharpen the end with a file or grinder to a point. Presto, you have created a tool to pry the most persistent weed out of crack or crevice. It works well in cushion plants, too, creating minimal disturbance of the roots of the desirable plant.

. . .

Come April and May, the perennial garden pushes up and out of the black compost with startling speed. It's time for spring-summer garden tending. When asters and phlox grow to about 2 feet, we shear them down to about half their height to prevent very tall growth, which is liable to topple in summer even with supports. It's time also for our large three- or five-legged collection of gridded supports to be set out. When done early, flowering stems grow through the grid, which becomes invisible by summer. Plants may lean on each other in friendly embrace, but with the support grid, they won't collapse onto each other after a heavy rain or with overhead watering.

Early May is time to say goodbye to hellebore flowers. By now, most of them lie underneath new foliage, their calyces swollen and heavy with almost ripe seed, just ready to burst and drop their load of a thousand new babies underneath their skirts. Sepals have turned green and have lost visual interest, except those beautiful black and slate flowers still showing off among yellow carex and hakonechloa. I am torn between beauty and future work weeding innumerable seedlings. We must remember that all open-pollinated garden seedlings are usually not the same glorious color as their parent, but incidental offspring, the result of careless pollination by bees in search of sweet nectar and pollen. Only a few will be as brightly colored as their parents. Most will be of a rather muddy shade.

Our summer irrigation is time-consuming and tedious since we need to conserve water, and yet I cannot look at a wilted plant without feeling as stressed as those drooping leaves. We make it easier with battery-powered timers installed at each faucet and connecting all hoses with quick-release couplers—a marvelous invention, coupling hoses with just a click. We use large oscillating sprinklers that can cover an area of 50 by 30 feet but are adjustable. We only irrigate from sundown to early morning to conserve water. With the density of planting and all the digging we do in our beds, drip irrigation is not feasible except in isolated areas.

During summer, much of our time is spent in the perennial garden. Delphiniums can be induced into a second, early fall blossoming by cutting spent flower stems to the ground and supplying them with an extra dose of fertilizer. Dahlia seed heads look like buds but with pointy ends—in contrast to the round shape of as yet unopened buds—and are nipped off daily. It extends the season of our mostly single-flowered specimens into fall. The spent flower spikes of penstemon, phlox, salvia, and others are cut for a second show on their laterals. We do all we can to lengthen the season of flowering.

At the same time, we like to keep overabundant self-sowers in bounds. Seed heads of thalictrums, astrantias, *Anthriscus sylvestris* 'Ravenswing', and others of their ilk are carefully cut and gingerly deposited into the wheelbarrow, lest they spill their seed along the way. Perennial borders are the most labor-intensive areas in any garden. Are you ready to give up your summer travels? Is there a better summer than spending July and August amidst your flowers? Winter is the time to flee, when gray and soggy skies threaten and icy winds blow.

. . .

At the end of summer, bulb catalogs arrive in the mail. I've learned to try to write down garden spots for new bulbs before the tempting catalogs arrive. Then, at planting time, in October and November, I have at least an idea what and where I would like to plant more, and I always want to plant more. So, I write in my notebook: more 'Casa Blanca' lilies here, or a patch of pink *Anemone blanda* there, and I write down location, or at least put it down in my ever-infallible memory, although Ernie might dispute the infallible aspect.

We use a mix of fish and bone meal, or bulb fertilizer, dug into the soil under the bulbs to give them a good start. Finally, the art of gardening includes the joy of anticipation and surprises, and a bulb planted in the wrong spot can always be moved!

Three-year-old seedlings of *Trillium kurabayashii*.

Three-year-old seedlings of faster growing *Trillium albidum*.

Four-year-old seedlings of *Erythronium revolutum*, ready to transplant into larger pots or the garden.

The Miracle of Seeds

An economical and entertaining method of acquiring plants that can be expensive and difficult to find is to grow them from seed. We have bought very pricey plants, tiny but irresistible, that looked forlorn planted in a large garden. They can be showcased in a trough, but, in the open garden we longed for not just one or two, but a big patch. Choice alpine gems such as some *Primula* or *Meconopsis* species are almost impossible to find as plants at any price. Those dark red *Trillium kurabayashii*, or the silver-leaved *Arisaema sikokianum*, or the *Paris polyphylla* with those long, slender, thread-like petals and bright red seed heads in the fall were just not readily available to us for purchase without breaking the bank. The answer was seeds, plus patience. We have grown thousands of plants from seed, yet the excitement and wonder when that first flush of green pushes up through the gravel is always new and cause for joy.

Being inveterate seed collectors, when we return from hiking trips to high, dry, western deserts and alpine areas, we often have acquired seeds for our chaparral or rock gardens, or obtained seed from one of the many plant societies. To start them, we mix a sterile potting mix called Black Gold All-Purpose Potting Soil at a ratio of 75 percent to 25 percent horticultural-grade perlite. If a fast-draining mix for seedlings is needed, we increase the percentage of perlite up to half. Once any seed is sown, to keep the seed in place and to stabilize the moisture, we cover the pots with about ¼ inch of chicken grit #2. Then we wait and hope.

As a general rule, plants from damp or woodland habitats like their seed sown fresh, or at least not dried out, while seed from plants of desert and dry environments need a warm, dry resting period before being sown into a moist compost-perlite mix. Composites should be sown in spring following the year of collection. If no seedlings appear the first year, we keep the pots for another year, because some plants, like trillium and paris, take two or more years to come up.

metric conversions and hardiness zones

inches	centimeters	feet	meters
¼	0.6	¼	0.08
⅓	0.8	⅓	0.1
½	1.25	½	0.15
1	2.5	1	0.3
2	5.0	2	0.6
3	7.5	3	0.9
4	10	4	1.2
5	12.5	5	1.5
6	15	6	1.8
7	18	7	2.1
8	20	8	2.4
9	23	9	2.7
10	25	10	3.0

Temperatures

$°C = 5/9 × (°F–32)$

$°F = (9/5 × °C) + 32$

Plant hardiness zones

To see temperature equivalents and to learn in which zone you garden, see the U.S. Department of Agriculture Hardiness Zone Map at planthardiness.ars. usda.gov/PHZMWeb/

For Canada, go to planthardiness.gc.ca/.

acknowledgments

Gardening is, in some ways, a very individualistic endeavor. The greatest peace and joy are found when we are puttering away in the garden, planting new plants, pruning, or even weeding. The cares of the world recede and we are aware of the basic elements—soil, sunshine, air, and water—and of being a part of Nature, not simply an observer. But gardening is also very much a communal activity, having a long and venerable history of which we are a part. We owe so much to those who have gone before us and to our fellow gardeners and nursery owners who have been an inspiration to us. Because of their multitude they must remain unnamed.

Many thanks go to those who have helped us with their knowledge and plant identifications: Linda Beutler, Mark Bloom, Paul Bonine, Roger Gossler, Russell Graham, Rick Serazin, Greg Shepherd.

The magical artistry of Doreen Wynja is clearly obvious to whoever picks up this book. With photography shoots once a month, and sometimes more, over the course of a year, her untiring devotion to this project cannot be acclaimed highly enough. We appreciate the many hours spent to capture the feel and mood of the garden.

Profound thanks, too, go to those who helped us begin, many years ago, with hellebores: Will McLewin (Phedar Nursery), Gisela Schmiemann, Judith and Dick Tyler (Pine Knot Farms), Kevin Belcher and John Massey (Ashwood Nurseries), Graham Birkin (39 Steps Nursery), John Dudley (Elizabeth Town Hellebores), and Hans Kramer (De Hessenhof Nursery). Their love and knowledge of the genus has been encouraging.

The reading and guidance by Cole Burrell and Lucy Hardiman were an invaluable help in the art of writing and in bringing this book to realization as a comprehensible whole. Tom Fischer, acquisitions editor at Timber Press, has a gentle but insistent voice of persuasion. Without that voice, this book would certainly not be in your hands. Thanks, Tom, for spurring us on. We also feel sincere and heartfelt admiration and appreciation of Ellen Wheat, responsible for transforming our awkward phrasing and sentence structure into what we hope will be a delightful read for all. We were charmed and enchanted by her magic.

resources

Societies and Groups

Alpine Garden Society
alpinegardensociety.net
AGS Centre, Avon Bank
Pershore, Worcestershire.
WR10 3JP
United Kingdom
Phone: 01386 554790
e-mail: ags@alpinegardensociety.net

The Society is for anyone interested in alpine plants, rock gardening, and rock garden plants—in fact, any small hardy plants and bulbs. Has quarterly journal, seed exchange, and online resources.

American Horticultural Society
ahsgardening.org
7931 E Boulevard Dr
Alexandria, VA 22308
Phone: 703.768.5700
e-mail: webmaster@ahsgardening.org

Dedicated to making America a nation of gardeners, a land of gardens. Has many varied resources for all types of gardeners, both online and in their magazine.

Arisaema Enthusiast Group
Arisaema-L: mailman.science.uu.nl/mailman/listinfo/arisaema-l

List for arisaema enthusiasts. Has annual seed exchange.

Snowdrops and Galanthophiles Group
on Facebook: https://www.facebook.com/groups/160399837333841/

Group for anyone loving snowdrops. Over 2000 members, many very knowledgeable.

Heavenly Hellebores Group
on Facebook: facebook.com/groups/eobiii/

Anything and everything hellebore related. About 5000 members worldwide, many very knowledgeable about the genus.

North American Native Plant Society
(and individual state native plant societies)
PO Box 84, Station D
Toronto, Ontario, M9A 4X1, Canada

A volunteer-operated registered charitable organization concerned with conserving native plants in wild areas and restoring indigenous flora to developed areas.

North American Rock Garden Society
nargs.org

NARGS is for gardening enthusiasts interested in alpine, saxatile, and low-growing perennials. Has seed exchange and online resources, as well as a quarterly journal.

Scottish Rock Garden Club
srgc.net/site

The club for people who love plants. Has seed exchange, online resources, weekly bulb blog and biannual journal.

Woodland Plants for Cold Climates Group
on Facebook: https://www.facebook.com/groups/627095910681586/

Over 5000 members worldwide with extensive plant knowledge about cold hardy plants f or shade conditions.

Our Favorite Mail Order Nurseries

Annie's Annuals
(carries many perennials, too)
anniesannuals.com
801 Chesley Ave
Richmond, CA 94801
Phone: (888) 266-4370 or (510) 215-3301

Supplier of unusual and choice varieties of annuals and perennials.

Cistus Nursery
cistus.com
22711 NW Gillihan Rd
Portland, OR 97231
Phone: 503-621-2233

Supplier of unusual perennials and trees with a specialty of xeric adapted. Large display garden.

Dancing Oaks Nursery
dancingoaks.com
17900 Priem Rd
Monmouth, OR 97361
Phone: 503-838-6058

Carries a host of unusual perennials, conifers, and deciduous trees mostly exhibited as mature specimens in their large displays gardens.

Gossler Farms
gosslerfarms.com
1200 Weaver Rd
Springfield OR 97478
P: 541-746-3922

Provides a host of very choice plants, many unavailable elsewhere, mostly shrubs and trees. Specialize in magnolias and fall color. Large display garden hosting a very choice magnolia collection underplanted with a host of choice shrubs, vines and perennials.

High Country
highcountrygardens.com
(mailing address only)
2438 Shelburne Rd, Ste 1
Shelburne, VT 05482
Phone: (800) 925-9387

"At High Country Gardens our mission is to improve the earth one garden at a time by offering unique plants that are drought resistant or native."

Joy Creek Nursery
joycreek.com
20300 NW Watson Rd
Scappoose, OR 97056
Phone: (503) 543-7474

Features species of Clematis, Dianthus, Fuchsia, Hosta, Hydrangea, Penstemon, and many other genera. There is a large display garden featuring many of their plants.

Pine Knot Farms
pineknotfarms.com
681 Rockchurch Rd
Clarksville VA, 23927
PHONE: 434-252-1990

Provider of just about every variety of hellebore on the market and grown very well.

Van Engelen
vanengelen.com
23 Tulip Dr
PO Box 638 Bantam, CT 0675
Phone: 1-860-567-8734

Provider of bulbs of all varieties at very reasonable prices. A $60 minimum per order. For smaller quantities, use their retail outlet, John Scheepers: https://www.johnscheepers.com/

McClure and Zimmerman
mzbulb.com
Phone: 800-883-6998

Provider of bulbs of all varieties.

a few of our most-used books

Beutler, Linda. 2004. *Gardening with Clematis*. Portland, OR: Timber Press.

Brickell, Christopher, and Judith D. Zuk, eds. 1997. *The Royal Horticultural Society A-Z Encyclopedia of Garden Plants*. New York: Dorling Kindersley.

Burrell, C. Colston, and Judith Knott Tyler. 2006. *Hellebores: A Comprehensive Guide*. Portland, OR: Timber Press.

Case, Frederick W., Jr., and Roberta B. Case. 1997. *Trilliums*. Portland, OR: Timber Press.

Chatto, Beth. 2000. *Beth Chatto's Gravel Garden*. New York: Viking Studio, Penguin Group.

Cubey, Janet, ed. 2013. *RHS Plant Finder*. London: Royal Horticultural Society.

Culp, David L. 2012. *The Layered Garden*. Portland, OR: Timber Press.

Darke, Rick. 2007. *The Encyclopedia of Grasses for Livable Landscapes*. Portland, OR: Timber Press.

Elliott, Jack. 1995. *Bulbs for the Rock Garden*. Portland, OR: Timber Press.

Gossler, Roger, Marjory Gossler, and Eric Gossler. 2009. *The Gossler Guide to the Best Hardy Shrubs: More than 350 Expert Choices for Your Garden*. Portland OR: Timber Press.

Gusman, Guy, and Liliane Gusman. 2006. *The Genus Arisaema*. 2nd ed. Portland, OR: Timber Press.

Hinkley, Daniel J. 1999. *The Explorer's Garden: Rare and Unusual Perennials*. Portland, OR: Timber Press.

Hinkley, Daniel J. 2009. *The Explorer's Garden: Shrubs and Vines from the Four Corners of the World*. Portland, OR: Timber Press.

Lloyd, Christopher. 1993. *Christopher Lloyd's Flower Garden*. New York: Dorling Kindersley.

Mathew, Brian. 1987. *The Smaller Bulbs*. London: B. T. Batsford.

Ogden, Scott, and Lauren Springer Ogden. 2008. *Plant-Driven Design*. Portland, OR: Timber Press.

Rice, Graham, and Elizabeth Strangman. 1993. *The Gardener's Guide to Growing Hellebores*. Portland, OR: Timber Press.

Steffen, Richie, and Sue Olsen. 2015. *The Plant Lover's Guide to Ferns*. Portland, OR: Timber Press.

Toomey, Mary K., and Everett Leeds. 2001. *An Illustrated Encyclopedia of Clematis*. Portland, OR: Timber Press.

van Gelderen, D. M., and J. R. P. van Hoey Smith. 1996. *Conifers: The Illustrated Encyclopedia*. 2 vols. Portland, OR: Timber Press.

Wiley, Keith. 2014. *Designing and Planting a Woodland Garden*. Portland, OR: Timber Press.

photography and illustration credits

Doreen Wynja: pages 6, 17 right, 21, 22, 24, 26 top and bottom left, 27, 29, 32 right, 34, 35 bottom, 36 bottom left, 37, 40 left, 42 bottom left, 44 left, 46, 48 right, 49, 50 top right, 58 right, 60, 63, 64, 65, 67 right, 68, 70 top center, bottom left, center, and right, 71, 72, 74, 75, 77, 79 bottom left and right, 80, 82, 83, 84 top left and right, middle left, center, and right, bottom center, 87, 90, 93, 94, 96, 97 top, 102 bottom right, 103, 106,108 bottom right, 110, 112 right, 114, 119 right, 120, 121 right, 122, 127 right, 129, 132, 133 right, 136, 137, 138, 139 left and center, 140, 142 right, 143 top right and bottom left, 144–145, 146, 147 top, 152, 154–155, 157, 160, 161, 164, 170, 171, 172 top left, bottom left and right, 174 left, 177, 179, 180, 183 right, 185, 187, 188, 190 left, 193, 196, 198 top left and right, 199, 200 left, 202, 205, 206, 208, 210, 211 bottom left and right, 213, 214, 215, 216, 225 top and bottom right, 228 top and bottom left, 229, 230, 241.

All other photographs are by the authors.

Endpaper illustrations by Mia Nolting.

index

Bryan DeVore

Marietta and Ernie O'Byrne are the owners of Northwest Garden Nursery in Eugene, Oregon. Formerly a retail nursery specializing in unusual plants, it is now a wholesale nursery specializing in hellebores. With a worldwide network of customers, the nursery has earned a reputation for producing some of the finest hellebore hybrids available today. The O'Byrnes' garden is renowned for its stunning combinations and variety of habitats, which allow Ernie and Marietta to experiment with a huge palette of plants. Marietta speaks regularly to audiences of passionate gardeners and has written for a number of gardening publications. You can visit the nursery's website at www.northwestgardennursery.com.